CONTENTS.

CHAPTER I.
Fifty Years Ago 1

CHAPTER II.
The Owenian Socialist Movement . . . 13

CHAPTER III.
The Anti-Corn-Law League and the Chartists . 26

CHAPTER IV.
The Concordium 40

CHAPTER V.
The Communist Propaganda . . . 53

CHAPTER VI.
Popular Literature Forty Years Ago . . 77

Contents.

CHAPTER VII.
The Chartist Movement 96

CHAPTER VIII.
The Great Petition 118

CHAPTER IX.
The New Organization 143

CHAPTER X.
O'Connor and the "Northern Star" . . . 169

CHAPTER XI.
Papers for the People 186

CHAPTER XII.
A New Phase of the Reform Movement . . 197

CHAPTER XIII.
Mission Work in Bethnal Green 210

CHAPTER XIV.
John Cassell and his Literary Staff . . . 226

CHAPTER XV.
Provincial Journalism and Journalists . . 239

FORTY YEARS' RECOLLECTIONS:

LITERARY AND POLITICAL.

BY

THOMAS FROST,

AUTHOR OF "THE SECRET SOCIETIES OF THE EUROPEAN REVOLUTION," "THE LIFE OF THOMAS, LORD LYTTELTON," ETC.

London:
SAMPSON LOW, MARSTON, SEARLE, AND RIVINGTON,
CROWN BUILDINGS, 188, FLEET STREET.
1880.

[All rights reserved.]

FORTY YEARS' RECOLLECTIONS.

CHAPTER I.

FIFTY YEARS AGO.

FIFTY years are not a very long period in the history of a nation, much less in that of the world, yet what mighty events may be crowded into them—what vast changes made in the social, political, and educational condition of a people! Looking back, for instance, upon the England of half a century ago, we have a retrospect which presents as strong a contrast to the present time as the infancy of an individual affords to the same person's mature years. So rapid has been the progress of the nation in mental development and political enfranchisement that men not yet old may look back upon the days of their boyhood as curiously and as wonderingly as their fathers did upon the age of the Tudors. Men who are yet but in the autumn of their days have seen the first rail laid of that mighty network of iron roads that now extends over the whole country; the first gas-lamp lighted in their native town; the first popular periodical, and the first penny newspaper; the first mechanics' institute; and the first Quaker and the first Jew admitted into Parliament. The generation that has attained manhood during the period which has been blessed with all these elements of a high degree of civilization, and many more, can form only a faint and inadequate conception of the times when gas and steam were known only as philosophical experiments; when popular periodicals were non-existent; and no newspaper was published at a lower price than eightpence.

Such was the state of things in this country when —now nearly sixty years ago—I first saw the light in the old, and then rather dull, town of Croydon, which, however, was a fair example of the towns of its class, urban centres of agricultural districts, before railways had connected them with the metropolis, or gas lighted their streets. I see it now, in my mind's eye, as it was then; with Whitgift's Hospital, dating from the reign of Elizabeth, and affectionately and reverently styled by my fellow-townsmen "the College," forming its most conspicuous architectural feature at the point at which it was then entered by the high road from London; and the bent old men and women sunning themselves in the prim little courtyard—a glimpse of which is obtained through the archway by which it is entered from the street. From that corner the long, narrow High Street stretched southward, dull rather than quiet, with here a slow grey-tilted carrier's cart, and there a Brighton stage-coach, stopping to change horses, with the scarlet-coated guard on the back seat, equipped with post-horn and blunderbuss.

The grey tower of the old church—then the only one in the parish—was seen over the roofs on the right, across a street leading to the slums of the Old Town; and, looking after the coach as it dashes off again to the sound of horn, the royal arms over the entrance of a substantial edifice of very red bricks, with a sign-board swinging from a beam across the street, proclaimed the principal inn—from the windows of which the Tory candidates for the representation of the county were wont to address their supporters. On the opposite side of the narrow street was the old butter market (now converted into a printing office) to which farmers' wives brought butter, eggs, and poultry, in that golden age of Tory-Radical politicians of Cobbett's school, when farmers wore linen gaberdines, as their forefathers had done since the days of Egbert, and their wives did not disdain to milk the cows, make the butter, feed the poultry, and collect the eggs. A little farther on, with the best of the sleepy shops on the right and the left, and over the way, was the local Capitol, where farmers stood on market-days behind their samples of corn on the ground floor, while above them the justices sat to hear charges of poaching and other rural offences, and the Court of Requests to adjudicate upon claims for small debts.

What could a country town want more?

In those days nothing; so at least thought the Croydonians of that period, who were eminently Conservative and unprogressive. There was little communication with the metropolis, and less with the neighbouring towns; and so much did the tradesmen confine their dealings to the town, that I remember hearing an old shopkeeper assert that, owing to the predominance of credit transactions, you might go from one end of the High Street to the other, and fail to get change for a sovereign. Coaches ran through the town daily, and the goods-traffic was conducted partly by carriers, and partly by means of a branch of the Surrey Canal, which had its junction with the Thames at Deptford. There were persons then living, however, who remembered the time when pack-horses were used, a mode of conveyance availed of even during the first quarter of the present century by smugglers, who travelled by night, through green lanes and woodland paths, from the coast to obscure nooks on the outskirts of the metropolis.

The police arrangements belonged equally to those "good old times," which every generation laments, but refers to a different period. The modern constable in uniform had not superseded by day the honest tradesman who, when his services were required, had to be sought (but was not always found) behind his counter or in his workshop, and by night the decrepid old man to whom the parish authorities entrusted the guardianship of life and property during the still hours of darkness, in order to keep him out of the poor-house, and whose many-caped coats and horn-lanterns used to afford such fun to juveniles when, in the Christmas pantomime, "Charlie" was upset in his sentry-box by the clown.

Gas and steam were discoveries which had been heard of only to be ridiculed. Many a chuckle I have heard over the absurdity of the idea of lighting the town with "smoke." Steam was a later innovation than gas, and yet found the inhabitants of the sleepy old town no better disposed to receive new ideas, for I remember a caricature in which men were represented as riding upon tea-kettles, with the steam puffing from the spout. The application to Parliament for the authorization of the railway which now connects the town with the metropolis and the coast was the signal for a general chorus of consternation and despair. Everybody, it was said, would go to London to procure the articles which they had hitherto purchased in the town, and the local shopkeepers would be ruined. All the villages below Croydon would send fruit and vegetables to London, and the market-gardeners would be ruined. The coaches and the carriers' carts would be driven off the roads, and horses would not be worth an old song.

Of course there was no local newspaper in those days, and the high price of the stamped journals of the metropolis precluded the possibility of their being very widely read. Penny publications were not yet in existence, and literary institutes and book clubs were equally unknown in that dull old town, where a man who could read and write was regarded as a scholar. The literature of the people consisted in those days of sixpenny books, in paper covers, in which were related the lives of famous highwaymen, or such stories as those of George Barnwell and Arden of Feversham, embellished with brilliantly-coloured folding plates. Until the first penny serial was issued by the Society for the Diffusion of Useful Knowledge, the only books I ever saw in my father's house, besides the bible and a few old school books, used by my eldest sister, were some odd numbers of Cobbett's *Register*, with the famous gridiron surmounting the first page, and a few pamphlets, amongst which I can remember reports of the trial of the Cato Street conspirators, and that of Sir Robert Wilson and others for aiding the escape of Lavalette from the Conciergerie.

Education was discouraged in those days by the upper classes, and scarcely appreciated by the middle and lower grades of society. When William and Robert Chambers began the issue of their popular and still existing periodical, which was closely followed by the first penny venture of the Useful Knowledge Society, and the National and British School Societies began to dot the darkened land with schools, a large proportion of the upper and middle classes regarded the efforts then being made to educate the masses with extreme disfavour. Elderly gentlemen shook their heads gravely, and expressed fears that, if the working classes were taught to read and write, it would soon be impossible to obtain servants. All the boys would desire to be clerks, and all the girls governesses, and the silver spoon classes would be able to find no one to clean their boots and make their beds. The first locomotive was not viewed with more fear and distrust than the first elementary school and the first penny periodical.

But the feelings with which the circulation among the masses of the driblets of knowledge supplied by the early popular serials was regarded by Tory squires and parsons were mild in comparison with the horror with which they viewed the newspapers which, because the working classes could not afford to buy journals bearing a threepenny stamp, appeared without it. No term of opprobrium was too strong to be applied to the unstamped newspapers, which comprised all the representatives of the working classes, and naturally were Radical in their general tone, and in their treatment of the leading questions of the day. Prosecution after prosecution, resulting in heavy fines and long imprisonments,[1] failed to suppress these pioneers of the penny press, which were printed and published with the greatest secrecy, distributed by a variety of devices, and sought by working men with an avidity that increased with the supply of the aliment and the risks that attended the procuring of it.

In such conditions little mental activity was to be expected in the smaller provincial towns, especially in the agricultural districts, where men's intellects are unsharpened by friction with their fellows as in the larger towns of the midland and northern counties. The thinking powers of that generation

---

[1] Henry Hetherington, with whom I was acquainted more than thirty years ago, and who was the proprietor and editor of the *Poor Man's Guardian*, estimated the number of persons sentenced to imprisonment for selling unstamped newspapers at five hundred; but Mr. Heywood, a Manchester bookseller, in a paper read before the Literary Club of that town, stated that the number was seven hundred and fifty.

were stagnant. In the towns and villages of the south men's minds seemed to be slumbering, until the puff of the steam-engine should awaken them. Political opinions scarcely existed. There was a great display of party feeling at elections, but the colour of a rosette, rather than difference of principles, distinguished one party from the other. Men called themselves Blues or Yellows, as the case might be; and the less they knew of the principles which the colours symbolized the more ready they were to fight for them.

I remember being roused from sleep one night, about fifty years ago, by the uproar created by the ceremony of "chairing" the successful candidates, who, of course, were Tories; for the single Whig candidate was in those days nearly always defeated in Surrey. Getting out of my bed, and flattening my nose against the window, I saw a long line of carriages, escorted by a dense mob, hoarse with shouting, in whose midst floated, at intervals, yellow flags and banners, their staves carried at every angle, and waving from side to side in a curiously serpentine manner, as their bearers described a line of beauty along the muddy street. It was the era of the agitation against the removal of the civil disabilities of persons of the Romish communion, and every dead wall and hoarding was scrawled with the motto, "No Popery."

But, though they grew excited over the fortunes of the Blues and the Yellows at election times, the Croydonians of that period did not ordinarily interest themselves much in the political questions of the day. When the contest at the hustings and the polling-booths had ended, as it usually did, in the return of a brace of Tory squires, they subsided into an apathy which had in it much of the selfishness evinced by a local coal and potato dealer, who, being questioned as to his political sympathies, replied, "I am for them that buy potatoes of me." I believe that the publication most read in the town in those days was a scurrilous little sheet of the *Paul Pry* class, issued by a printer named Tickle, whose office was a miserable wooden house at the corner of Middle Street and Bell Hill, since converted into a lodging-house for tramps.

There was, however, a little knot of Radicals in the town, who, abused, ridiculed, pointed at, denounced as dangerous characters, as they were then, formed the nucleus of the local Liberal party of the future. The most active members of this much-abused band were Charles Thompson, a clerk in the service of a brewer named Harman; a journeyman tailor named Washford, who was the pioneer of the much-needed movement for reforming the management of the Whitgift charities; and my father, who then carried on the business of a tailor in the High

Street. These men worked quietly, but with considerable success, for the dissemination of their principles; and the political ferment of 1831, to which the French revolution of the preceding year contributed in no small degree, found a large number of the working classes prepared to join in the agitation for "the Bill, the whole Bill, and nothing but the Bill," namely, the Reform Bill introduced that year by the administration of which Earl Grey was the chief, and Earl (then Lord John) Russell the leading exponent in the House of Commons.

Like all masses of men who have just awakened to a dim consciousness of their rights, but have not yet learned even the rudiments of politics, the "great unwashed"—their descendants will pardon a term borrowed from Cobbett—were prone to noise and violence; and, even if the Radicals of the smaller towns, such as Croydon, had not been, in that respect, far in the rear of Birmingham and Manchester, they could not be expected to prove an exception to the rule. The rejection of the Reform Bill by the House of Lords excited them to such a degree of fury that, when the Archbishop of Canterbury, who had voted against the Bill, visited the town shortly afterwards for the purpose of consecrating St. James's church, they received him with howling and hooting, mobbed him at the church, and pursued him with reviling and menaces on his departure.

As I was, at that time, only in my tenth year, I can record of that period, and the events of the few preceding years, only such imperfect recollections as my memory retained in after-life. It was not until ten years later that I became connected with the Press, or with any political organization; and I shall, therefore, commence my recollections of the Socialist and Chartist movements of forty years ago with a new chapter.

CHAPTER II.

THE OWENIAN SOCIALIST MOVEMENT.

Forty years ago the minds of vast numbers of the thinking portion of the working classes throughout the most highly-civilized countries of the world were filled with ideas of the perfectibility of human nature and the reconstruction of society upon the basis of universal liberty, equality, and fraternity. Ever toiling for a mere subsistence—seeing everywhere around them poverty, vice, and misery, in startling contrast with wealth and luxury, excluded from the rights of citizenship, smarting under the inequalities and anomalies of the laws enacted by the representatives of a small minority of the people, without hope of relief from any action of the governing classes—they embraced with ardour the theories of moral and social regeneration which were at that time in course of active promulgation, in England by Robert Owen, in France by Cabet, Proudhon, and Constant, and the disciples of those elder revivers of the day-dreams of the Illuminatists,

St. Simon and Fourier, in Germany by Weitling and Albrecht.

I was about sixteen years of age, and knew nothing of the Owenian ethics and social economy, when I was attracted to a gathering of Owen's South London disciples at the Tivoli Gardens, a respectably-conducted place of recreation at Norwood, partly by curiosity as to what Socialists were like, and partly by the announcement of a brilliant display of fireworks. The Socialists proved to be persons whose appearance and manners did not render them in the slightest degree remarkable, and their founder a little, benevolent-looking, quiet-mannered gentleman in an ordinary suit of black. A short address was delivered by the philanthropist, and then dancing on the lawn commenced, concluding when darkness began to settle upon the pleasant scene, and gave the necessary background for the pyrotechnic display, the culminating effect of which was the motto, in letters of fire, "Each for all, and all for each."

I had just been reading Coleridge's "Religious Musings," and the brief address in which the philosopher of New Lanark had set forth the principles of his new constitution of society sent me to the poem again. The scheme of the philosopher seemed to be the due response to the aspirations of the poet. At that time, however, it interested me chiefly in its metaphysical aspect. It was not until after I had read the grand and wondrous poems of Shelley, two or three years later, that my mind became impressed with the connexion between the influence of circumstances in the formation of character and the new organization which Owen desired to give society.

Socialism, as expounded by Owen, seemed to present a perfectly practicable solution of a problem which had been for some time working in my mind, namely, how the progress of the physical sciences and mechanical arts could be made most conducive to the happiness and well-being of the people. Without the means to such end, and the knowledge to apply them, civilization would, it then seemed to me, be but the ripening of society into rottenness. This was clear to my mind from what I knew of the condition of the masses, and of the prevalence of every form of social evil, which, towards 1842, seemed to be approaching its climax.

In those days no small amount of moral courage was required in the man who avowed himself a Socialist. There were social difficulties of no mean order to be encountered by men above the artisan grade who adopted the political creed embodied in the People's Charter. I was once refused as a tenant by a Tory landlord, solely on that ground; and I believe that many persons of the middle classes had the same opinion of a Chartist that Johnson had of a punster. But, if a Chartist was suspected of designs tending to the wholesale infraction of the eighth commandment, a Socialist was held in horror as certainly capable of violating the entire decalogue. I am not sure, even at this day, it is unnecessary to assure the reader that Socialists of the Owenian school did not advocate either a plurality of wives or the promiscuous intercourse of the sexes, and were not all atheists; for, forty years ago, the most erroneous ideas prevailed with regard to these points, owing to the falsehoods and misrepresentations with which the press and the pulpit then teemed; and since Owen's death, or rather since the collapse of the Hampshire experiment, the philosopher and his teachings have been forgotten.

Undoubtedly there were some ardent disciples of Owen who would fain have anticipated the legislature by constructing a new code of marriage and divorce for themselves. I remember receiving a letter from the late James Napier Bailey, a well-known Socialist lecturer of that day, in reference to a communitive project presently to be mentioned, in which one of the questions asked was: "What arrangements do you propose with regard to marriage?" But all that was contended for by Owen was a law of divorce, and a tribunal for its administration that would be accessible to all classes of the community. That such a law and such a tribunal was needed in the interests of morality and social order was known to every one who was aware of the sin and misery engendered by the legal indissolubility of marriage, especially amongst the working classes; and it was not contended, even by those who were opposed to the principle of dissolubility, that the power of obtaining a divorce should depend upon the ability of the wronged individual to expend from 500*l.* to 1000*l.*, which was the cost of a private Act, then the only means by which a divorce was obtainable.

Parliament has since conceded, in principle at least, all that Owen ever demanded, and for his advocacy of which he was denounced by the late Bishop of Exeter, in his place in the House of Lords, and by the then Bishop of Norwich, and many of the clergy, from their pulpits, as the promulgator of the detestable system of promiscuous intercourse. There is not one line of Owen's works which affords the slightest foundation for this charge, which his clerical calumniators would have known to be false if they had been half as earnest in endeavouring to ascertain the truth as they were zealous in striving to blacken the philanthropist's reputation.

There was just as little ground for branding the Socialists as a body with the stigma of atheism.

So completely was perfect freedom of religion identified with the system propounded by Owen that several of the residents at Harmony Hall were regular worshippers at the neighbouring parish church; and the governess of the infant school of that community was a member of the Society of Friends. But nothing was too bad to be believed of Owen and his disciples; and so eager were the newspaper editors who desired to be regarded as supporters of religion, morality, and social order to circulate rumours tending to discredit Socialism and its founder, that a false and libellous paragraph, which appeared in a periodical publication entitled, *The Antidote to Socialism and Infidelity*, edited by a person named Brindley, was copied, without inquiry, into almost every newspaper in the three kingdoms. It stated that the operations in Hampshire had been suspended, and that Owen had fled from Harmony Hall, taking with him 15,000*l.*, which he had obtained by false representations from two elderly spinsters. The whole story was a malicious invention, which the libellers were made to retract by threats of legal proceedings. Harmony Hall was then rapidly approaching completion, and Owen had just gone to reside there, having previously lived in London.

Great was the outcry raised when Lord Melbourne introduced Owen to the Queen, and the venerable philanthropist placed in the sovereign's hands a copy of his "Book of the New Moral World." Who can tell the extent to which that unwarranted clamour influenced the minds of those who believed the minister guilty of the deviation from virtue attributed to him by the promoters of the action in which Grantley Norton was the plaintiff. Probably there were many thousands of persons who conscientiously believed Socialism to be what it was proclaimed in the press and the pulpit, a system behind which all took refuge who wished to cast off the restraints of society, and make free with their neighbours' wives and chattels. Few persons who were not Socialists read the *New Moral World*, and there was no corrective, therefore, to the falsehoods and misrepresentations which were sown broadcast by the press.

Does the reader remember the course adopted by the conductors of a certain exponent of middle-class Radicalism, then boasting the largest circulation among all the weekly newspapers, to create a "public opinion" hostile to the Poor Law Amendment Act? If not, a few words will explain it. There appeared, every week, a column headed "Horrors of the New Poor Law," and under this head were collected all the cases of suicide, infanticide, and death from privation, which had occurred during the week. Very similar to this was the course pursued by that and other newspapers in dealing with Socialism. It was a very common device for complainants and witnesses to say of a person charged with larceny, wife desertion, or almost any other offence, "He is a Socialist;" and reports of all such cases had the side-head, "Effect of Owenism," while the term "Socialist Marriage" was commonly applied to connexions unsanctioned by law and religion.

The press took no notice of Socialism so long as there was no opportunity of vilifying its professors, therein acting in the same manner as then and subsequently with regard to the Chartist movement. So far as any information could have been gleaned from any newspaper, the Harmony Hall experiment could not have been supposed to be in progress. A significant contrast to this silence was afforded by the alacrity with which, when the building operations were partially suspended, for want of funds, in the summer of 1842, almost the entire metropolitan and provincial press, without distinction of party, copied the false statement of an evening journal, that the Socialist establishment in Hampshire was finally broken up, after an expenditure of 37,000*l*., that the workmen were all discharged, and that Owen had left the place. This was not enough to satisfy the self-constituted guardians of moral and social order, and hence the calumnies of Brindley.

All this clamour was excited by an endeavour to improve the moral and material condition of the people by the application of the co-operative principle to the erection of dwellings in which all the social and domestic arrangements, aided by all the resources of science and art, should be directed to that end. Owen contended that the character of each individual is formed by the circumstances by which he is surrounded, and that therefore the provision of the best conditions was the necessary prelude to the formation of the best type of character. Actuated himself by the purest philanthropy, he thought that he had only to show what he designated the rational system of society in actual and successful operation to inspire all the statesmen of the civilized world to adopt it, and to enlist in its favour the governing classes everywhere. To that end he sacrificed a large private fortune, and devoted the best portion of a long and useful life, reaping in return only calumny and disappointment.

The Hampshire experiment interested me very much. The communitive life seemed to me the perfection of political, social, and domestic economy, and to present equally the best conditions for a truly Christian life, and the realization of that state of which so many sages and poets have dreamed in all ages, in which sin and sorrow should be no more, ignorance and want be unknown. I longed for association with kindred spirits in community, corresponded with Owen and others, sought admission to Harmony Hall; but it was not to be. There were thousands of others as eager as myself to make trial of the communitive life as presented in Owen's system, and whose claims had precedence of mine. The experiment eventually collapsed—not, I believe, through defects inherent in the system, but owing to the difficulty which those who attempted to reduce it to practice experienced in adapting themselves to its requirements. Upon this point I shall have a few observations to make in relation to some similar experiments upon a smaller scale.

Forty years have elapsed since that time. The Rational Society has long ceased to exist; its founder has passed away from this world, and experienced, I trust, that "beautiful surprise" which a Christian lady of considerable literary attainments anticipated for Harriet Martineau; the system which he advocated has no longer an exponent, either in the press or in the lecture-hall. Yet, in practice, and without the name, Socialism flourishes more widely and strongly than ever. Though we never hear of it, the results of its teaching are everywhere around us, and its fundamental tenet, "man is the creature of circumstances," may be recognized in all the legislation of the last quarter of a century. This state of things is the more remarkable from the fact that it has been brought about without any consciousness on the part of those who have created it that they were acting upon the principles which called forth such furious hostility forty years ago.

The affiliation of the co-operative factories and workshops of Lancashire and Yorkshire is indisputable; but no one suspects of Socialism the promoters of public baths and wash-houses, improved dwellings for the working classes, reformatory and industrial schools for juvenile offenders, district and separate schools for the children of paupers. Lord Shaftesbury, the denouncer of Owen in 1840, is one of the most active and influential promoters of these ameliorations; and assuredly his lordship is no Socialist, Owenian, or of any school. A little consideration must satisfy every impartial mind, however, that the institutions mentioned have sprung directly from the conviction that man *is* the creature of circumstances, and that by them his character is formed.

So numerous have been the reforms of this kind during the last twenty or thirty years, that they can be ascribed only to the gradual awakening of society to the conviction that there was much more in Socialism than its critics were willing to acknowledge while its advocacy was associated in the public mind with atheism and immorality. Repudiating it as a system, social reformers have availed of its teachings, and sought to improve the minds and morals of their fellow-creatures by ameliorating the conditions amidst which they are placed. But, as none of these reforms have been effected by Owen and his disciples, the connexion between the thought and the work has escaped recognition by society.

In one solitary instance alone has Robert Owen been publicly acknowledged by a person not holding his views as the originator of any one of the many reforms which he indicated or inaugurated. About twenty years ago, when a petition was presented to the House of Lords on behalf of a gentleman named Wilderspin, on the ground that he was the founder of infant schools, Lord Brougham rose to correct the statement, informing the House that the first infant school was devised and established by Robert Owen for the children of the workers employed in his extensive cotton-spinning establishment at New Lanark.

But, whether the obligations of society to Owen are acknowledged or not, the fact remains that statesmen have been acting for more than a quarter of a century upon the fundamental tenet of Socialism, and drawing, in all their plans for the amelioration of the condition of the people, upon the foreshadowings of one whom they formerly regarded as an impracticable ideologist or a dangerous anarchist.

CHAPTER III.

THE ANTI-CORN-LAW LEAGUE AND THE CHARTISTS.

It was while working in a printing office in Croydon, and with ideas of the reconstruction of society and the perfectionation of human nature working in my mind, that I met, for the first time, two men, each remarkable in his way, though one never emerged from the obscurity of his humble position as a shoemaker, and the other set his mark upon the age, and died with the reputation of a statesman.

In the autumn of 1842, a period of serious commercial depression and of severe distress amongst the working classes, the late Richard Cobden made a tour through the agricultural districts, accompanied by Thompson, Villiers, and other notabilities of the Anti-Corn-Law League, for the purpose of converting the farmers to his views of the policy of free-trade in corn. In carrying out this purpose he was met by the difficulty that the farmers could be addressed only in the market towns, and that the urban working classes were, as a rule, opposed to the aims of the League. Though none had better reasons for desiring cheap bread than the artisan and the labourer, there was a wide-spread impression that low quotations on the Corn Exchange meant low rates in the labour market; while among the Chartists the view taken of the free-trade movement was, that the agitation required for the attainment of free-trade in corn would suffice for the success of the movement for parliamentary reform, which would then enable them to obtain the repeal of the Corn Laws, the enactment of the Ten Hours Bill, and every other measure requisite for their well-being, without the agitation that would otherwise be the necessary preliminary to every reform in which they were interested.

There was sound sense in this view, but it did not move the Leaguers, who were interested in only one of the many ameliorations desired by the masses. As a consequence of its adoption by the industrial classes, however, the Leaguers were opposed at several of the towns which they visited with a resolution, moved and seconded by working men, affirming the repeal of the Corn Laws to be a reform which could easily be obtained when the majority of the people possessed the franchise, and the free-trade movement to be one which should, therefore, be subordinated to the agitation for parliamentary reform.

Croydon exhibited at this time evidence of social progress and intellectual vitality which had not been visible twenty years before. Since the railway had been made, so far from being ruined, it had grown rapidly in every direction, and mental progress had advanced in the same ratio as commercial activity. There was a flourishing Literary Institution, a Book Club, and other indications of more active intellectual life than had characterized the inhabitants in the days of oil lamps, stage coaches, and rampant Toryism. Newspapers were found in every place of public resort, and there was a large and increasing demand for the numerous low-priced publications which had sprung into existence during the last ten years.

The Radical party was represented by a branch of the National Charter Association, an organization which had been in existence about five years. The members enrolled in Croydon were not very numerous, but they were thoroughly imbued with democratic ideas, and active and earnest in their dissemination. The men who openly and actively take part in any political movement are always a few compared with those who hold the same views, but do not declare themselves; and Radicalism had progressed in the town in the ratio of the intellectual progress which had been achieved in the ten years preceding Cobden's visit.

The gathering on the open space behind the Corn Market on that occasion was the first demonstration of the kind at which I assisted. It was market-day, and I found the broad area dotted with groups of farmers of various grades, from the holder of a thousand acres down to the brown-faced men in gaberdines who brought poultry, butter, and eggs to the market. The shopkeepers of the town were too busily employed behind their counters to attend the meeting, and the hour being an inconvenient one for the working classes, not then liberated by the early closing movement, the townsmen were represented chiefly by the few artisans who either had nothing to do, or deemed it their duty to lose half a day's earnings for the sake of supporting their principles.

The Leaguers had just ascended the waggon which had been drawn up against a corn warehouse to serve as a platform, when the dark clouds which had lowered ominously since noon began to discharge their aqueous contents, and umbrellas went up like a sudden growth of gigantic mushrooms, as well on the waggon as over the heads of the crowd below. A consultation seemed to be held by the Leaguers as to the course to be pursued under these adverse conditions; but there were no symptoms of retreat on the part of the crowd, and the indecision was ended by General Thompson stepping forward, and saying, as he extended one hand towards the throng below, "If it doesn't rain there, it doesn't rain here." Loud applause greeted the remark, and the proceedings were commenced.

Cobden's address was listened to with great attention, and though there were some expressions of dissent when he had concluded, applause greatly predominated. When the resolution in favour of free-trade had been moved and seconded, the waggon was mounted by a man with a black linen apron twisted round his waist, and another wearing a fustian jacket and corduroy trousers.

"Name!" cried several voices in the throng, on its becoming evident that the man with the black apron intended to address the meeting.

"Blackaby! James Blackaby!" was called out in stentorian tones by the man in the fustian jacket, who, as I learned from a mechanic standing near me, was a sawyer named Hodges, the secretary of the local branch of the Chartist organization.

Whether Jem Blackaby, as I heard him familiarly called by a knot of working men near the waggon, was a good orator or an indifferent one I am unable to say. I have heard many terribly eloquent orations from working men, and listened to many very poor speeches in the House of Commons. I am bound to record that the man with the black apron made a fair start, but he had not delivered himself of more than a dozen lines when Cobden interrupted him with a petulant assertion that "this man," who had "put an apron on that he might look like a working man," was a hired agitator, who had followed him all through the country for the purpose of disturbing the meetings which he addressed.

"No, no! We know him," was shouted from below; and the man with the black apron raised his voice, protesting that he had not slept a night out of the town during the last two years, and denouncing the interruption as illiberal and unfair.

Cobden persisted in his statement, however, asserting that he had seen "the man" at every meeting he had addressed, always with the black apron round his waist, and always with an amendment in favour of the famous "six points." In this he was certainly mistaken; and it is to be regretted, for his fame's sake, that he should have persisted in an assertion which, if it had concerned an individual in his own sphere, he would either not have made, or have retracted on its inaccuracy being affirmed by those present. His persistence had the desired effect. Blackaby was known only to a few of the crowd around the waggon, and the representatives of the agricultural interest, whatever they may have thought of free trade, were not disposed to support a Chartist—a designation which in those days was regarded by the middle classes as a synonym for anarchist. The latter had so much the advantage of numbers over those who supported him that Blackaby was soon overpowered by clamour, and, after a vain endeavour to obtain a hearing, he contented himself with reading his amendment. It was seconded by the sawyer, but, on being put to the meeting, was supported only by the knot of working men near the waggon.

The rain abated during the uproar, and before sunset it had ceased. I was passing, in the evening, a beerhouse in the outskirts of the town, when I heard one of a group of mechanics, who were smoking their pipes at the door, inform his companions that Jem Blackaby was in the parlour. The movement that was made in the direction indicated convinced me that Jem was a local celebrity in his own sphere, and I followed the men into an apartment filled with a blue haze of tobacco smoke, through which I recognized the man of the black apron. Having got through the arguments which he had not been allowed to advance at the meeting, he was now engaged in an animated discussion on the merits of the system of society propounded by Robert Owen.

Seated opposite to him, I was able to observe Blackaby with more attention than I had bestowed upon him in the afternoon. He was a spare man, about the middle height, with a slight stoop at the shoulders, contracted probably by constantly bending over his work of boot-making, which might also be chargeable with a marked narrowness of the chest. His face was one of those strongly-marked countenances which, once seen, are never forgotten. He was very far from being even ordinarily good-looking, and yet both his aspect and his manners were prepossessing. Dark hair—the habit of which "shocky" describes more accurately than "curly"—hung in elf-like locks about a furrowed forehead, the height and breadth of which did not exceed the average, though the facial angle was almost perfect. Beneath his dusky locks, which he often put back with his hand while speaking, shone a pair of fine dark eyes, full of expression, and constituting the sole redeeming feature of a sallow countenance, thickly pitted with the traces of small-pox, and almost destitute of whiskers.

Taking part in the discussion myself, I soon discovered that he was very fairly acquainted with Owen's system, which he debated, from his own point of view, with rare impartiality, and with a fluency of expression, a command of language, and a degree of argumentative ability, not often met with even amongst those who have enjoyed the highest educational advantages. We became acquainted that evening, and, in the course of many subsequent years, I passed many an agreeable half-hour in the shoemaker's garret, talking by turns of politics and poetry. He might have been the prototype of Alton Locke, for he was a poet as well as a politician, and I shall have something to say concerning his poetical productions in another chapter.

His poetical proclivities came out one day through a diversion which he made from a conversation on the land question by observing that his pronunciation of the word "contrary" differed from mine, and asking me, with the air of a man desirous of learning, whether there was any other authority than custom for making it short, with the accent on the first syllable. He reminded me that both Shakespeare and Milton made it long, with the emphasis on the second syllable, and quoted passages from "Henry IV." and "Samson Agonistes" in illustration.

I thought of Bloomfield and Gifford, and wondered whether I had found another budding poet in a son of Crispin. Remarking that his occupation must be favourable to mental cultivation, I mentioned the Suffolk tailor's son and the Cornish cabin-boy—examples which elicited the confession that he also had, in his leisure, cultivated the acquaintance of the Muses, though he did not anticipate that his name would ever be inscribed on the muster-roll of fame. He had never, he said, had an opinion of anything that he had written that would have warranted an endeavour to obtain publicity for it, but he would be glad to hear my opinion. He then produced some stanzas, written upon a sheet of foolscap, which, though they could scarcely have been put in competition with the poems of the better known bards who have combined the making of verses with the making of boots, had the true ring in them, and a hundred years previously might have caused the author's name to be inscribed amongst British poets. But poems and essays which sufficed to make their authors' fame in the last century are now so numerous that they are read only to be forgotten.

The circumstances under which I first met Blackaby—the antagonism of the wealthy Leaguer and the poor Chartist, the successful endeavour of one of the privileged order to prevent one of the unenfranchised from obtaining a hearing—were a fitting prelude to the unfortunate strike and outbreak of 1842, which followed close upon the incident I have related. Throughout the autumn, mills were closed, mines empty, furnaces blown out. Hungry men paced in thousands through the streets of the manufacturing towns of the midland and northern counties, and congregated by torchlight on the dusky moors in their vicinity, to listen to the exciting harangues of their leaders, who told them, in stern language, of their wrongs. Blood was shed and property destroyed in several of the manufacturing towns of the north. The Guards were sent down from London to suppress a movement that seemed to threaten a revolution; but the crowds that attended them, both on their departure and their arrival, testified plainly that their sympathies were with the insurgents.

The letters of the late Sir Charles Napier, who commanded in the Midland Military District, have since revealed how critical was the situation and how great the embarrassment of the Government. There was the greatest dread that such a conspiracy might exist as burst harmlessly in the autumn of 1839; and while every magnate who knew himself to be unpopular besieged the Home Office with applications for military protection, a threatening demonstration in one place, an attack on a mill at another, an incendiary fire at a third, harassed the authorities, who knew not where the dreaded blow might be struck, nor how to distribute their forces to meet it.

Though the Chartists did not suggest the suspension of labour that, beginning at Ashton-under-Lyne, spread all through the manufacturing districts, their movement acquired from it a considerable impetus, the trades union delegates assembled in conference at Manchester having adopted, by a large majority, a resolution approving " the extension and continuance of the present struggle until the People's Charter becomes a legislative enactment," and pledging themselves to give, on their return to their respective localities, "a proper direction to the people's efforts." The Government were therefore not without grounds for their fear of a dangerous and wide-spread revolt.

Though the rural districts exhibited none of the excitement so strongly displayed in the midland and northern counties, the authorities were on the alert wherever the Chartist organization had been introduced, not knowing how far the danger manifested elsewhere might have extended. Was it not at the little town of Newport, in Monmouthshire, that the conspirators of 1839 fired the train that was intended to produce a revolutionary explosion at Birmingham, the reverberations of which should be felt throughout the kingdom?

In Croydon this watchful and expectant attitude of the authorities had some ludicrous results. In consequence of a Chartist meeting in the Old Town having been announced by a bill headed "Men of Croydon! are the working classes to be goaded into rebellion before their grievances are redressed?" the police were instructed to keep a sharp look-out for seditious or inflammatory bills. Some laughter was one day created by a short-sighted constable rushing across the High Street to read an announcement which he fancied was headed "Chartists! read, pause, and consider!" The bill really announced a gathering of "teetotallers," and the constable had read *Chartists* for *Christians*.

When the fears of the authorities were approaching the climax, the inspector of police was led to believe, "from information he had received," that a case of muskets had been brought into the town by one of the local carriers, and deposited in the house of a gunmaker in the High Street, to be used in a revolutionary outbreak. Inquiries made of the carrier elicited information which seemed to confirm the inspector's secret intelligence. The police thereupon made an irruption into the suspected premises, and there found the case, but not the muskets. The contents of the case were fowling-guns, which had been sent to be repaired, and concerning the ownership of which satisfactory information was given by the consignee.

I did not at that time connect myself with the Chartist organization. The poetry of Coleridge and Shelley was stirring within me, and making me "a Chartist, and something more," as the advanced reformers of that day were wont to describe themselves; but as yet I, with many more, occupied towards Chartism the position which the professors of that political creed held towards the Corn Law repealers. We believed the demand for the Charter to be a just one, but the goal of our aspirations was far beyond it, and we were unwilling to waste our strength in agitating for anything less than the reconstruction of the entire fabric of society.

CHAPTER IV.

THE CONCORDIUM.

The Socialist movement gathered new strength from the misery and despair which prompted and followed the strikes and tumults of 1842, which seemed a conclusive demonstration of the irrationality of the competitive system. Advances upon the line of march indicated by Owen were made by seceders from political and religious bodies which opposed Socialism. Chartists who held republican views as to the future of government separated from the main body, whose aims were strictly constitutional, and, under the name of Charter-Socialists, advocated a model republic on the basis of the People's Charter and Socialist institutions. Earnest Christians—who saw in the establishment of such institutions the fulfilment of Hebrew prophecies, and the realization of the Gospel proclaimed by Jesus in the synagogue at Nazareth, yet shrank from enlisting under the banner of an avowed materialist, as Owen then was—organized themselves as Christian Socialists, declaring their conviction that the communitive system of society was the only basis on which the precepts of the Gospel were practicable.

Here and there individuals combined the advocacy of communitive institutions with some crotchet of their own, and gathered around them a few disciples—repelled from Owenism by the materialistic teachings of its founder and most of those who followed him, or impatient of the slow progress which, to their sanguine minds, it seemed to be making in the direction of practical operations. One of these movements originated, in 1842, with the disciples of James Pierrepont Greaves, a psychological mystic, who died at Ham, near Richmond, in the early part of that year, when his mantle was held to have fallen upon William Oldham, a neighbour and follower.

The experiment, which was commenced at Alcott House, on the verge of Ham Common, shortly afterwards, was conducted on principles materially different to those which were being worked out at Harmony Hall, with the exception that both were under that *bête-noir* of the Charter-Socialists, the paternal system of government. Greaves and his disciples maintained, in diametrical opposition to Owen's views, that the existing generation could not be perfected, or even appreciably improved, since no amount of education or moral training, or any other external condition, could repair the defects of birth. The regeneration of society could, in their view, be brought about only individually, not by acting on masses; and the process must be internal, not external—thus reversing the formula of Owen. Holding this view as a fundamental tenet of their faith, they adopted the communitive system only as a means of attracting men and women of loveful natures and cultivated minds, in order that by and through them the mass of society might be leavened, and a new moral world evoked out of the chaos of old and effete institutions.

To this little group of earnest workers for the regeneration of society my mind turned when I found the doors of Harmony Hall practically closed against me. I opened a correspondence with the Pater, as William Oldham was styled by the brotherhood, and received an invitation to dine at the Concordium, and confer with him as to the harmony of our views and the practicability of realizing my wishes, while obtaining a glimpse of the life which the Concordists were living. To this invitation were appended the following observations, called forth by my having intimated that I contemplated entering the marriage state, which I did about eight months afterwards:—

"You are not sufficiently acquainted with our habits, diet, &c., to act in so important a matter without previous knowledge of all things relative to a residence in the Concordium. It will be well, if you think any further of it, to come and talk over the matter, particularly as you have thought of another still more important step, which will involve all that concerns your future progress and destiny. This step I hope you will defer taking, for the present at least. If you wish well to the female portion, or to the whole family of man, you will pause before you entangle yourself in this oppressive net, this dangerous, delusive, lustful engagement. If you favour us with a call, we will talk the matter over, and see if we cannot come to some clear idea of its real character.

"You are some years too young for such an engagement, and the young woman too old for your age;[1] but this is not of so serious a nature as the unrighteous connexion itself. A pretended union, or a supposed union, sanctioned by the corrupt law of the land, is a complete delusion, only to be deeply regretted in long tedious years of repentance, when the consequences press heavily upon mind and body, upon pocket and children, upon wife and husband; when sickness and disease are multiplied by three, perhaps by ten, and

---

[1] I was then within two months of completing my twenty-second year, and the difference between our ages was just nine months, the lady being the elder.

poverty and distress fill up the bitter cup of remorse and dismay. The hoax which the priest palms upon the deluded pair is found out but too late, when behold! the married couple find they have been decoyed into a pit of misery, out of which nothing but death can deliver them. They then awake from the dream of ease and happiness, and look around in vain for deliverance; whilst nothing but pain, crying, ugliness, filth, and discontent respond to their call.

"Fearful as this may appear to your vivid fancy, it is not nearly so appalling as the consequences of early marriages generally. But enough for the present. Let me see you, when we can take a view of the best side of the question. I should not object at all to your bringing your betrothed friend with you, and helping you to live a happy, affectionate, wise, and useful life in the Concordium, apart from all that disgraces and disgusts the virtuous and the good.

"By word of mouth we can enter more minutely and clearly into the subject, whilst by writing we cannot explain it at all correctly, and therefore are very liable to misunderstand each other."

Undeterred by this extraordinary epistle, and wishful to learn more of the singular community from whose chief it emanated, I steamed up the Thames to Richmond on a bright September morning, and thence had a delightful walk to Ham Common. Arrived at the Concordium, I was received by a young man, clad in a chocolate-coloured blouse, and displaying a profusion of hair and beard, the former parted in feminine fashion—two characteristics which I found to be common to all the brotherhood. By him I was introduced to the Pater, a little elderly man, of ascetic aspect; and then, as dinner was already on the table, sat down to a repast, not exactly of—

> "An overflowing store
> Of pomegranates and citrons, fairest fruit,
> Melons, and dates, and figs, and many a root
> Sweet and sustaining;"

but of rice, sago, and raisin puddings, potatoes, carrots, and turnips—raw as well as cooked, the Concordists not only being strict vegetarians and water-drinkers, but believing that the process of cooking deprived fruits and vegetables of the etherialising properties which they attributed to them, in accordance with an idea which may be found in Shelley's "Revolt of Islam," in the description of the feast of the liberated nations.

After dinner I had some conversation with Oldham on the points of difference between the Concordist system and that of Owen. These I found to be greater than I had been aware of, or was prepared for. I was disconcerted by the discovery that celibacy was recommended until the nature of the individual had become regenerated; and marriage was then to be placed under restrictions similar to those which prevailed among the Rappists of New Harmony, in the United States. Self-denial and asceticism were enjoined, as a means of rehabilitating the fallen nature of man; and the use of animal food was regarded with as much horror as by the votaries of Brahma.

"Would you kill? Would you shed blood?" Oldham asked, on my expressing dissent from his extreme vegetarianism, which extended even to the exclusion from the table of butter, milk, and eggs.

I felt that I was not sufficiently etherialised for fraternization with the Concordist brotherhood; so, after hearing an afternoon lecture from William Galpin, who had recently seceded from the Rational Society, and having a walk in the garden with Colin Murray Campbell, the young man by whom I had been received, I took my leave of them.

With Campbell I maintained for some time an epistolary discussion on marriage, vegetarianism, and other essentials of the Concordist philosophy; but our correspondence resulted in the conversion of neither. Winter proved, however, that the regimen of the Concordium was not adapted to extra-tropical regions. The Ham Common communitarians found raw carrots and cold water unendurable when the snow lay thick upon the ground, and the thermometer was below zero. Most of them returned to the outer world.

"Our family is getting rather small," Campbell wrote to me in November. "This is not to be wondered at, considering the strict discipline of the place, and the unfit race of men to become so good as to all at once take to such a line of action. Then again we have not stopped short of this, that, or any kind of food, but are trying every kind that can simplify our living. Uncooked we shall, I think, soon arrive at. I wish you to mark the progress we are making. Every step towards simplicity is good, and has Divine sanction."

The simplicity to which he referred had at that time become a mania with some of the sections into which the regenerators of society were divided. Galpin and some others, who had located themselves on one of the five farms comprised in the Harmony estate, on the sale of that property, not only adopted the vegetarian and water-drinking system, but also abandoned the use of shoes and stockings; and I believe there were some who would have revived the nudity of the Adamites of the middle ages, if they could have done so without bringing themselves under the lash of the law.

Campbell left the Concordium soon after writing the letter just quoted, and located himself in

London, whence he wrote me a long letter, the following passage of which shows that his mind was in a very unsettled state upon more matters than one :—

"It was the fortune of war! Yes, the war of the mind. I cannot call it peace. If I did, I should lead you astray. From the facts of the case, many were the thoughts, and hard was the struggle, that did for some time sway my mind previous to my coming to the determination I have; and now it is only half come to. The peaceful home among those who really love you! And then the thought of coming to the old work, for little system—grumbling and fretting the year round. The thought of remaining in this state! yea, the thought is distraction! the fact damnation, to all that can be called noble, loveful, and free! However, the change has been made, for better or for worse.

"You, my brother, may think this change hasty, and without thought for the future. Not so; although my mind is not yet settled upon any immediate step, yet I think to remain in town a short time. Then, no doubt, I shall let you know what my thoughts are upon future operations. Believe me, this old state will not do long for me, and I must change. This in many things is not at all unlikely, yet in such as this it is not so likely. It is not the thought of a day, but the quiet thought of years.

"There are few at the Concordium at this time. It is expected that with the flowers the number will increase. This is the hope with the Pater."

Few of the commoners did return with the flowers. Some of them subsequently emigrated to Venezuela, under the auspices of the Tropical Emigration Society. The Venezuelan Government was at that time offering free grants of land, and the society named was formed for the purpose of colonizing a certain tract on the co-operative system, for the development of which such grants were thought to afford peculiar facilities. The society had for its organ a small publication called the *Rising Sun*, which advocated vegetarianism and the communitive life, both of which advances were deemed by the editor and his friends to be more practicable in Venezuela than in England. It had a very brief existence.

James Elmslie Duncan, by whom that publication was conducted, was a young man of ardent temperament, and greater aptitude for the poetic than the practical side of the Utopia idea, and sufficiently erratic to incur the suspicion that his mind was not so well balanced as his friends could desire. He may be remembered by many as the young man, with long fair hair, parted like a woman's, and shirt-collar *à la Byron*, who was arrested during the Chartist agitation of 1848, for creating an obstruction in Bishopsgate Street by reciting some verses of his own composition; and again on Tower Hill, when, the excitement which he displayed causing him to be detained, a loaded pistol was found in his coat pocket.

After my visit to the Concordium I indulged the idea that, by making known my views and wishes, I might associate with myself some twelve or fifteen persons of both sexes, holding the same views, who might aid me in establishing a communitorium on the basis of the ethical and economic principles promulgated by Owen, but on a more humble scale than Harmony Hall, of the success of which the inadequacy of the results to the cost had caused me to become doubtful. My idea was to lease a large house, in some quiet and healthy locality in Surrey or Kent, with sufficient land to produce all the vegetables and fruit we might require; and there to carry on the occupations for which there would be an internal demand, such as tailoring and shoe-making, and to which work in the garden would afford an agreeable and healthful change.

I found, however, that, though the believers in social regeneration were numerous enough, few of them were sufficiently imbued with the earnestness of purpose, singleness of mind, and thorough unselfishness, necessary for the reduction of Utopian ideas to practice. With Socialism as with Christianity, the conviction of the intellect is more common than the change of the heart. Colin Campbell wrote to me on this subject as follows:—

"Many of my social friends in London have been speaking about you, and I was able to state my thoughts upon the subject of such an affair as you are about starting. Let me here remark, that many will communicate with you who have got the money, and who, in a monetary point of view, may be right, but deficient in morals and intellect; for remember, this old rotten state of society has been brought to its present state by men, and it exists by the joint assistance of such. And who can doubt when such a stream of vice and wickedness has been running for so many years, those that may apply will be more or less touched and tainted by the pollution, either in one, or two, or perhaps all the three—intellect, morals, and physical nature? This you may depend, and it will require you to be very careful whom you select to commune with.

"After you have got into working, you will not be so likely to make mistakes; but you must make sure of good and true men and women to make the start with, or down you will most assuredly go, and sorrow for your pains. This might damn your hopes for life. All should join from the purest motives, no individual end coming before the universal end you ought to have in view. Let your little band, never mind how small, cast themselves at once upon the Universal, and deliberate what is best to be done. The uniting of persons in this family way is, in my mind, very like what I should like to see individuals in the marriage state united by, that is, that each of the parties should have worshipped at the Universal, and that in faith, hope, and love, before their union could be what I would call a true devotional marriage—that each should be entirely independent of each other, except in those points where love of the purest kind took possession of them. This, my friend, is the pure state of mind that I think parties must possess before they are fit to enter upon the list of the truly married, or into the social family arrangements.

"Accept this, in great haste, from one who admires your onward march. May glorious satisfaction of the most exalted kind be with you."

The announcement of my projected experiment brought me into correspondence with several men of cultivated minds, and great enthusiasm in the cause of social progress, who were at that time contemplating, or actually engaged in, similar experiments. But divergences of aim of one kind or another separated me from all of them, and the dream of planting an Atlantis among the breezy hills of Surrey was not realized.

CHAPTER V.

THE COMMUNIST PROPAGANDA.

My interest in the great problem of the reorganization of society continuing unabated, notwithstanding the failure of the various attempts that had been made in England, France, and the United States to reduce to practice the societary systems of Owen and Fourier, I was led by considerations of the existing condition of the different schools and sects of social reformers to contemplate the production of a journal which should serve as a record of progress for all of them, without being the special organ of any one of them.

The Rational Society was on the verge of dissolution, owing partly to financial embarrassments, and partly to internal dissensions, the latter arising from the difficulty of managing the affairs of Harmony Hall in a manner that would reconcile the rights claimed by the residents with the interests of the whole body. The former considered themselves entitled to elect their governor; while the latter maintained that, as they had contributed the funds wherewith the community had been established, the governor should be elected by their delegates, assembled annually in congress. The branches were agitated at the same time by differences about their local government; one section contending for the paternal system which was favoured by Owen, and the other standing up stoutly for democracy.

The various denominations of social reformers were so little known to the world which they desired to remodel, that the present generation retains only a dim and imperfect recollection of the Socialists, applying that designation to the disciples of Owen, and knows nothing of any other of the half-dozen similar organizations that existed in the United Kingdom alone in 1845. At the time when I conceived the idea of a general representative of Communism in the press, there existed, in addition to the Rational Society, which was very efficiently represented by the *New Moral World,* the Concordium, which had still a few commoners; the Little Bentley community, mentioned in the preceding chapter, as having been founded by William Galpin, who had been a draper at Southampton; the Communist Church, organized on a pantheistic basis by a gentleman named Barmby; the Charter Socialists, who deferred practical operations until the masses should have obtained their political rights; the Tropical Emigration Society, by whose instrumentality the Communistic Paradise, idealized by Etzler, was to be created in the wilds of Venezuela; and the White Friends, seceders from Quakerism, who had adopted the communitive system on religious grounds, and, with the confidence of faith, and the earnestness of their sect, had organized themselves in two communities, one on Usher's Quay, Dublin, the other at Newlands, a mansion and park in the vicinity of the Irish capital, and once the residence of the unfortunate Lord Kilwarden.

Each of these societies, with the exception of the Little Bentley family, had had its special representative in the press, the *New Age* being the organ of the Concordists, the *Communist Chronicle* of the Communist Church, the *Model Republic* of the Charter-Socialists, the *Rising Sun* of the Etzlerites, and the *Progress of the Truth as it is in Jesus* of the White Friends—all of monthly issue; and the last decidedly unique in journalism, and worthy of preservation as one of the curiosities of literature. All these had ceased to be published in 1845, having failed to obtain a sale that would even cover the cost of production; and I calculated that, if the various bodies which they had represented would send their reports of progress, &c., to me for insertion in the journal which I contemplated, there would be a remunerative circulation to start with.

I communicated with some of the gentlemen to whom I had become known two years previously, when endeavouring to organize a communitive experiment in Surrey, and received from them an amount of encouragement that I thought would justify me in incurring the risk of publication. But, before arrangements could be made for the production of the journal, it was necessary that I should secure a certain amount of literary assistance. The dead exponents of Communism had been conducted by men who had originated, or taken a prominent part in, their respective movements; and they were assisted in their several apostolates by contributors and correspondents of some literary ability. Some of these I hoped to enlist, especially Goodwyn Barmby, who, besides being a writer of remarkable originality, was in correspondence with Cabet, Weitling, and other leaders and directors of the Communist propaganda on the continent, a record of which I desired to make a leading feature of the new journal.

I had had some correspondence with Mr. Barmby while engaged in my endeavours to found a community in Surrey, at which time he was conducting a similar experiment at Hanwell, called the Moreville Communitorium, which, however, was not attended with success. A gentleman by birth and education, he had devoted his fortune and energies to the propagation of the Communistic theory of society, which he believed to be not only in harmony with the Christian system, but its completion, the crowning of the edifice. He had offered, some time before, to gratuitously translate Morelly's "Code de la Nature," a work of Communistic tendencies, for any publisher who would produce it at his own risk; and thinking that the translation would constitute an attractive feature of my contemplated publication, I proposed that he should execute it for me.

Mr. Barmby responded by endeavouring to impress me heavily with a sense of the difficulty of the work I proposed to undertake, and proposing that, instead of venturing upon the issue of a new paper, I should aid him in reviving the *Communist Chronicle*, which might be made to serve the same end. The question of the translation was left in abeyance. An appointment followed, and I met the founder of the Communist Church for the first time. I found him a young man of gentlemanly manners and soft persuasive voice, wearing his light brown hair parted in the middle, after the fashion of the Concordist brethren, and a collar and necktie *à la Byron*.

In a long and interesting conversation on the position of the Communist movement at home and abroad, and the prospect of such a journal as I contemplated attaining a remunerative circulation, it was made clear to him that I possessed facilities for its production which did not exist elsewhere, and to me that he commanded certain requisites of success in which I was deficient. He was acquainted with Wilhelm Weitling, who was then in London; had correspondents in Paris, Lyons, Lausanne, Cologne, New York, and Cincinnati; and was conversant with the whole range of Utopian literature, from Theopompos and Euhemerus, to Weitling and Albrecht.

The religious difficulty, which was destined to be a source of much misunderstanding, did not then come to the surface. Perhaps, while I was calculating that my control of the paper would enable me to secure the preponderance of my own views, my clever chief contributor was consoling himself for his subordinate position with the reflection that the necessity of his coadjutorship would give him all the influence that he could desire in the direction of the journal, while he would have none of the risk.

Mr. Barmby blended with the Communistic theory of society the pantheistic views of Spinoza, of which Shelley is in this country the best known exponent. By clothing the pantheos idea in the language of Christian theologians, he attracted to him, from time to time, members of the more obscure sects—Swedenborgians, Millenarians, Southcottians, White Quakers, and the like, the doctrines of all being ingeniously reconciled by him with the fundamental tenets of the Communist Church, which he announced as the continuation and completion of Christianity, and the all-embracing organization into which all churches and societies were ultimately to be absorbed.

I foresaw that, while these views might attract to the Communist movement some of the more advanced minds among the sectaries whose distinctive doctrine was the near approach of the Millennium, the realization of the New Jerusalem, or the advent of a Newington Shiloh, they would repel the Owenian Socialists, to whom I was chiefly looking for support, having regard to their enormous numerical preponderance over all the other sections of communitive social reformers, and in anticipation of the dissolution of the Rational Society, then on the verge of bankruptcy, and the cessation of the *New Moral World*. The advantages to be derived from our co-operation caused us, however, to amalgamate with more cordiality and unanimity than might have been expected.

The business arrangements being entirely under my control, I announced the revival of the journal as a weekly, instead of a monthly, publication, reduced in size one half, and in price from threepence to a penny. Under the direction of Mr. Barmby it had been published by Cousins, whose shop in Duke Street, Lincoln's Inn Fields, was at that time one of the chief emporia of the literature of free thought. Believing that Hetherington was more favourably disposed towards Communism than Cousins, and knowing that he had made sacrifices to the popular cause in the resistance to the newspaper stamp duty, besides being one of the organizers of the Working Men's Association, which had prepared the way for the People's Charter, of which he was one of the authors, I transferred the publishing department to him.

Instead of the "Code de la Nature," it was decided that the leading feature of the new series should be a translation of Weitling's "Evangile des Pêcheurs Pauvres," which had created in Germany a sensation equal to that which had been produced in France by the publication of the "Paroles d'un Croyant," of Lamennais. By one of the frequent changes of mind to which Mr. Barmby was subject, I never received this translation; but a series of "Studies on St. Simon, Fourier, and Owen," from the French of Louis Reybaud, which had been commenced in the monthly series, was resumed, and Mr. Barmby commenced, in an early number, an original philosophical romance, entitled "The Book of Platonopolis."

This was a vision of the future, a dream of the rehabilitation of the earth and of humanity; of Communisteries built of marble and porphyry, in which the commoners dine off gold and silver plate, in banqueting-halls furnished with luxurious couches, adorned with the most exquisite productions of the painter and the sculptor, and enlivened with music; where steam-cars convey them from one place to another as often as they desire a change of residence, or, if they wish to vary the mode of travelling, balloons and aërial ships are ready to transport them through the air; where, in short, all that has been imagined by Plato, More, Bacon, and Campanella, is reproduced, and combined with all that modern science has effected or essayed for lessening human toil or promoting human enjoyment.

Correspondence and reports of Communist progress were important features of the new organ of the movemeut. Reports were received every week from the little groups of the Communist Church, which had been formed in various metropolitan and provincial districts, and occasional communications from friends as yet unorganized, as well as from the Etzlerites, the Little Bentley family, and the White Friends. The foreign record was especially interesting, as, while at least one London daily had its foreign correspondence written in the Strand, we had veritable living correspondents in

Paris, Cologne, Lausanne, New York, and Cincinnati. Cabet exchanged his journal, *Le Populaire*, with us, and from an American editor we received the *Herald of Progress*. It was in our columns that the earliest intelligence of the revolt in Galicia appeared; and in them alone was reported the debate in the Swiss Diet, on the petition of the clergy and the landowners of Vaud for the suppression of all Communist societies, the dismissal of all public functionaries affiliated to them, and the expulsion from the country of all the alien members, a large proportion of the initiated being Germans.

The dissolution of the Rational Society, consequent upon its bankruptcy, occurred shortly after this commencement of my journalistic career, and seemed to me to offer the opportunity that I had anticipated for extending the circulation of our paper. Mr. Barmby, who was in communication with Mr. Buxton and Mr. Isaac Ironside, two of the most influential members of the society, appeared to share with me this anticipation.

"From all I hear," he wrote to me, "the *New Moral World* has no chance of surviving more than two or three weeks longer. Its death will be our gain. We shall inherit some hundreds of additional subscribers by its demise."

All the property of the society was sold shortly afterwards for the benefit of the creditors, and the copyright and plant of the *New Moral World* was purchased by Mr. James Hill, who had formerly conducted a small publication called the *Star in the East*, and designed his new venture to be the organ of a co-operative scheme of his own devising, which, however, came to grief. It was alleged by Mr. Fleming, the editor, that the copyright was the property, not of the Society, but of Robert Owen; and, in order that the Socialists might not be deprived of an organ pending the settlement of the disputed title, he brought out a journal called the *Moral World*, exactly resembling in size and form the paper with which he had ceased to be connected. It had, however, a very brief existence.

The time had now come for us to make an endeavour to obtain the support of the Socialists for our journal; but with it came also the intervention of the religious difficulty. With the Socialists, religion was an open question, though most of them were deists or materialists; and the way to have gained their support would have been, that it should have been so regarded by us, as had been my wish from the first. But my colleague, though naturally desirous of increasing our circulation, aimed at doing so by drawing the Socialists into the pale of the Communist Church; and this was an end very unlikely to be attained. Pantheism is not easily "understanded of the people," and, as presented to them by Mr. Barmby, it must have puzzled them to discover whether it was atheism in disguise, or a new reading of the Bible which they had rejected.

With the view, however, of giving a new impetus to the Communist movement, and thus increasing the circulation of the journal, we announced a project for establishing a communitorium in the little island of Sark, to be called the Caxton Communitorium; and, immediately afterwards, leaving the correspondence on this subject to be conducted by me, my colleague commenced a propagandist tour of the midland counties, visiting the groups, delivering lectures, and distributing tracts. Before he started on this mission, I received from him a letter, some passages of which I quote, to show the nature of the practical operations that were then contemplated.

"On Saturday," he wrote, "I had an interview, for the fourth or fifth time, with James Hill, on the very subject thou mootest in thy letter, only with a more favourable horizon. Since I last saw thee, as thou hast learned from the *Chronicle*, a portion of the Tropical Emigration Society has seceded from the main body on Communist principles, and, through their chief officer, connected itself with a group of the Communist Church. Now this society intends to establish a home colony, to gather its members together previous to being draughted off to Venezuela. The colony to be on a scale for twenty-four families, or about a hundred and twenty individuals. Union being strength, as soon as I heard of this project, I thought of uniting ours with it. On inquiring into the matter I found that the Venezuelan friends wished to locate near London; and, if I could join thyself and others with them, I should, from the fact of the increased power of associated numbers, prefer it to an immediate Channel Island community, although I hope to assist in organizing one there, and in a thousand other places, before I sleep the last sleep.

"Not only in location, but in the means of association also, was there a difference between my project and that of the Venezuelan emigrants' home colony. I anticipated a community. They want community in Venezuela; but only economic, and, in some respects associative, congregation here. They looked to an old building society for their lodging. I recommended them Hill's new one; and on Saturday last introduced the subject to Hill himself. It now remains for me to see how these two parties will work together. If they co-operate, I shall recommend a group of the Communist Church to form a third party in the matter in connexion with the publication of the *Communist Chronicle*, and until such a time as a more perfect community would be organized. Indeed, if the *Chronicle* was there, I should probably take a room for occasional residence in the establishment myself, and promote the issue of a Communist paper currency, and other matters. I must wait, however, and take no premature step in the matter.

"With regard to other observations in thy letter, art thou prepared to subscribe thyself a member of the Communist Church? Recollect that neither a materialist nor a spiritualist can be a member of that Sacred Future of Society. Its very name implies the contrary. Consequently, for many, probationary steps like the proposed union with the Venezuelan Emigration Society—so far as their home colony is concerned, I mean, and probably with Hill's machinery—would be desirable. Moreover, it must not be forgotten that there are two communities in Ireland, which approximate more than any other yet existing to the ideal the Good Spirit has given me to display."

The failure of my own attempt to organize a community, the collapse of the Hampshire experiment, and of the Fourierist phalansteries in France and the United States, to say nothing of the Hanwell and Ham Common communities, rendered me exceedingly anxious concerning the practical operations that were contemplated by my colleague, whose views on the subject appeared to be vague and indefinite, and of whose means of realizing them

I knew only that he had inherited a small estate at Yoxford, in Suffolk. The projected community seemed to be receding from view, like the illusory water of the African deserts, while the divergence of his views from mine was becoming more and more obvious in the contents of the journal.

There are no dates to any of his letters, but the epistle from which the following passages are extracted appears to have been written shortly after the one last quoted, and in answer to my expressions of anxiety concerning the Sark project:—" Others in connexion with me were not prepared sufficiently to embrace the perfect communion of the Communist church, but might have taken rooms, and congregated in one of Hill's groups. Consequently, it appeared good to me that these imperfect elements should be united, even upon a transitionary plan, connecting themselves, but in no wise preventing ulterior arrangements among more perfect Communists. These latter could find a more congenial home, either in the Irish communities, or in those that, through various means, I elsewhere hope to be instrumental in constructing.

"Among these I have proposed a community of printing and agriculture in the Channel Islands, to be commenced next spring, provided, of course, I can find before that time the proper materials to compose it. If, however, a congregation of approximate Communists took apartments in Hill's group, whether the Channel Island community was established or not, I should probably take a room for occasional residence in that establishment. In that establishment I should of course be an individual renter, or rather lodger, in common with the other members, no community or local government that I know of being understood in the case—Hill's plan being, as far as I understand, a plan for simply furnishing apartments in a united habitation to individuals for a certain payment, based upon the scale of life annuities, and ineligible to be conveyed in community. Of course the residents in such a habitation might work in common, and share products in common; but the house and land would not be the property in common of themselves, but that of the National Land and Building Association; and should any of our members die, their places might be filled up by that Association with individualists. Consequently, congregation, but not communion, is its proper mission. Nor did I consider it—except for the purposes of the former, in which light I thought and Huntington looked at it—in preference to the Communist Church."

Mr. Barmby was, in this matter, more practical than I usually found him, and expressed his views more clearly than he had ever done before. But he was mistaken with regard to my estimation of Hill's association; and on the higher question touched in these letters, he was as cloudy as ever. There would have been no difficulty in understanding his reminder, "that neither a materialist nor a spiritualist can be a member of that Sacred Future of Society" the Communist Church, if the sentence had stood alone. Had he not given the world a paraphrase of the Lord's Prayer, in which God was addressed as the great Creative Power, which "as Spirit does father us, and as Matter does mother us?" But how does this idea harmonize with the statement in the same letter that the communities of the White Friends—disciples of Fox, *plus* white garments and the communion of goods—approximated more nearly to his ideal than to any other yet existing?

Of course, as he observed in the second letter, of the accordance in degree of the Irish Communists with his own views he was the best able to judge; but others than himself had the right to receive a full and clear exposition of those views. It was the misfortune of those who accepted him for their leader, that they never knew the goal to which he was leading them. Viewing his erratic flights in the past by the light afforded by his career in later years, it would seem that, while endeavouring to found a church which should be "the Sacred Future of Society," he was really still groping towards the light, and seeking for something which eluded his search.

This is not an uncommon state of mind with earnest inquirers after truth. It was my own for some years, both before and after the period of which I am writing; but there was this difference between Goodwyn Barmby and myself, that I rested at the end of every stage, while he hurried on, with a zigzag course, in a manner which made it ever doubtful whether he would be found at the point where he had been heard of last.

The prospect was thus dubious, overcast with perpetually shifting clouds, and mists that dispersed only to gather again, when my colleague commenced the propagandist tour that was to result in the planting of groups of the Communist Church in all the towns of the midlands and the north. His reports were at first very encouraging. From Coventry, where he commenced the propaganda, he wrote:—"The work goes on bravely. The Bedworth lecture-hall was literally crammed. I am happy to say that I have united around our work here the remnants of the Christian Co-operators and the Socialists. The *Communist Chronicle* will more than quadruple its circulation in future in Coventry." From Birmingham he reported, about a fortnight afterwards,—"I am likely to become a popular preacher here. It is therefore my duty to remain at least a fortnight longer. I am already engaged for two lectures and two sermons."

Crowded lecture-halls and pleasant tea-parties brought no increase of circulation, however, notwithstanding the reported accession of numerical strength in every place that was visited. In the meantime, the Channel Islands project made no progress, and the divergence of our views became every week more evident. Neither in politics nor in religion were we in accord. He advocated the paternal system of government, I the democratic. "Neither democracy nor aristocracy," he wrote, "have anything to do with Communism. They are party terms of the present. In the future, governmental politics will be succeeded by industrial administration." In the present, however, it was not clear to me that men, even in small bodies, would submit to autocratic rule, however sugar-coated with a paternal aspect.

That danger loomed in the future. The more immediate evil was the doubting and misunderstanding created by Mr. Barmby's expression of the ideas of Spinoza and Shelley in language that would not have been inappropriate in a parish church, though it would assuredly have passed over the heads of a large proportion of the congregation. In arranging for him to continue to edit the paper, I had not intended that it should remain the special organ of the Communist Church. I wished it to be conducted on broad unsectarian principles, and would therefore not have objected to the exposition of Communist views on the basis of Pantheism, if Mr. Barmby had not chosen to present them, so based, in language calculated to mislead the majority of those to whom they were addressed.

Before deciding whether I would abandon the propaganda altogether, or conduct the paper independently, I communicated with some of the chief promoters of the movement, with the double aim of obtaining a clearer view of its position and prospects, and of ascertaining the extent to which the teaching of my colleague was appreciated by our readers. In the latter object I did not succeed, and the responses upon the former point were far from encouraging. Mr. Henry Hoy, the reporter of the Poplar group, wrote as follows:—

"I regret that there should not have been a proper understanding in reference to the *Communist Chronicle*, as I am of opinion with thyself that it might have been made to pay its expenses, and the breaking up of the Rational Society might perhaps have been made to have aided the same, had proper steps been taken. It does not appear that works of its character have ever been made to be very profitable. They are in advance of the age as far as their tendency goes, though the want of such as a medium by which to convey to all parts of the globe the sentiments that animate us is felt to be a real want."

In a second letter from the same gentleman, a wish was expressed that an arrangement could be made by Goodwyn Barmby and myself for the continuance of the publication, "because," said the writer, "I believe that it would bear more evidence of being a love-labour than any other that we have at the present day; for, unfortunately, they are all more or less intent upon making it a profitable affair. Not that I object to a publication being self-supporting or paying; such I believe it ought to be. Thy labour-love-offering is an acceptable sacrifice, and I hope that arrangements will be made to give the public the benefit of it. I regret that I am not in a position to incur the responsibility of making such arrangements, but will do what I can to bring it about, as I am quite certain that nothing can be more moderate than the remuneration thou namest, and think that steps should be taken for securing such a valuable co-operator in the cause of Progress as thyself."

Though the majority of the replies that I received had a discouraging tendency, I still cherished the idea of enlisting the support of the Socialists. The *Reasoner*, then recently commenced by Mr. Holyoake, was occupied chiefly with the diffusion of

Secularism; and the *National Reformer*, which, under the direction of James Bronterre O'Brien, had been for some time a vehicle for the expression of advanced views on political and social questions, had lately ceased to appear. I knew that the *Communist Chronicle* would also become extinct when I ceased to bear the cost of production, and I could not conceive the idea that there were not Communists enough in the United Kingdom, Owenian or otherwise, to support a single exponent of their views and record of their progress.

I determined therefore to proceed, and gave Mr. Barmby notice of my intention to terminate the arrangement under which the paper had been revived, at the same time announcing the immediate appearance of the *Communist Journal*, as a monthly advocate of the Communitive life and record of Communist progress at home and abroad. Mr. Barmby informed me that he regarded the title which I had chosen as an infringement of his copyright, and forbade me its use in a highly characteristic document, sealed with a seal of portentous size, engraved with masonic symbols, in green wax, green being the sacred colour of the Communist Church.

Disregarding this interdict, I issued my first number at the date on which it had been announced to appear; and, in the hope of gaining some support from the disciples of my late colleague, as well as from the Socialists, I gave a prominent position to an article in which were set forth the grounds of the difference between us, his various publications being quoted to show that he had promulgated inconsistent views of the Divine nature, and that the tendencies of his recent articles in the *Chronicle* were contrary to the tenets of the Communist Church, as expounded by him elsewhere. Hence a schism, and increased antagonism on the part of Mr. Barmby, resulting in the cessation of the *Journal* after the second issue.

Mr. Barmby's efforts to continue the publication of the *Chronicle* without my co-operation were equally unsuccessful, only two or three numbers being issued, and those at irregular intervals, after the rupture. "Much as an organ in the press is wanted by the Communist Church," he wrote to me some time afterwards, "it wants one only that shall be directly and supremely, I do not say exclusively, its organ, and under the control of its administration." This it never obtained, and in a very few years it had passed into the category of extinct Utopias. The religious views of its founder subsequently underwent a further development, and he is now a minister of the Unitarian Church at Wakefield.

Communism died out in England very rapidly.

We are not a gregarious people, and there are very few of us who would not prefer a cottage and a garden in individual possession, to a dormitory and common rights in the most splendid communistery or phalaustery that has ever been imagined. The Co-operative movement, with its various applications of the principle upon which it was based, drew into it all the more practical and less imaginative of the thousands over whose minds Communism had for a time exercised a potent charm. The comparative prosperity resulting from the development of free trade converted those whom Communism attracted only by the glowing prospect of material amelioration which it offered, and who formed the residuum of the movement.

The fewer thinkers and dreamers retained their faith in Utopia perhaps, but they abandoned the distinctive characteristics of their respective sects and schools, ceased to expect the realization of their day-dreams of the future in the present century, and directed their powers to the accomplishment of more practicable, and therefore more immediately useful reforms, if less lofty in aim, than the regeneration of humanity and the reconstruction of the social fabric.

CHAPTER VI.

POPULAR LITERATURE FORTY YEARS AGO.

At the time when I finally withdrew from the Communist propaganda, the taste of the masses with regard to mental aliment had undergone a change for the better, while the number of readers, as a consequence of the efforts made during the preceding fifteen or twenty years for the diffusion of education, had received a considerable extension. It will be obvious that popular literature, in the fullest sense of the term, could have no existence while the majority of the people were unable to read; while a desire for books must, in the earlier stages of a nation's education, be even more rare than the ability to read them.

No longer ago than the commencement of the second quarter of the present century readers were very few proportionately to the population, even among the lower grades of the middle class, and no editor of a periodical dreamed of addressing either them or the working class. Popular literature, regarded from this point of view, consisted of stereotyped editions of wonderful narratives and stories culled from the old dramatists, published by Fairburn or Bysh, at sixpence, in paper covers, and embellished with highly coloured folding plates, depicting the most sensational incidents of the story. Some of these were abridgments of standard works, such as Robinson Crusoe; but the greater number were such as could be given entire within the number of pages to which the printer was limited.

It is necessary to a right understanding and correct appreciation of the penny serials which received their impulse from the education movement that set in strongly half a century ago, that we should know something of the publications which they superseded. The prominent favourites of the rising generation of that day were the wonderful lives and adventures of Friar Bacon and Dr. Faustus—known to opera-goers and readers of Goethe by his right name of Faust—the venerable history of the Seven Champions of Christendom, some selections from the Arabian Nights, and an abridgment of the Memoirs of Baron Trenck. Readers of a riper age, but not mentally capacitated to appreciate a Radical newspaper, frowned upon the stories which had delighted them in their boyhood, stigmatized them as "lies and rubbish," and preferred true stories, generally narratives of crime, or the lives of notorious criminals.

These stories formed the staple reading of the masses when the grey-haired men of the present day were boys. Here and there might be a studious artisan who, before the cares and cost of a family pressed hard upon him, had acquired a quarto edition of Hume and Smollett, or Blomfield's "View of the World," with plate illustrations, in shilling numbers; or a radical shoemaker or tailor, whose desire for enlightenment as to his rights and his wrongs led him to devote his leisure to the study of Paine and Cobbett; but students were, as they still are, the minority among readers, and the majority wanted only to be amused.

The supply of better books than were then accessible to the working classes and that large section of the middle class which comprises the lower grades of the shopkeeping interest only needed a demand to be forthcoming, however; and the demand was being prepared on a large scale by the establishment of elementary schools all over the country, through the agency of the National and British School Societies. Enterprising publishers began to dream of standard works issued at prices within the means of every one, and therefore to be sold by tens of thousands. Constable projected, in 1825, though the idea was not carried out until two years later, a series of reprints, which he was confident would, in half a dozen years, "make it as impossible that there should not be a good library in every decent house in Britain as that the shepherd's ingle-nook should want the salt poke." But his great intentions and sanguine predictions were not fulfilled. The books which were to have had a place in every house were issued, during a period of commercial depression and industrial distress and discontent, in shilling numbers; and though some of them had a large sale, they were bought only by readers whose education and means were far above those of the masses.

The Society for the Diffusion of Useful Knowledge started with the same high aims, and, in their earlier issues, made the same mistake. The scientific treatises which constituted their first venture were far too abstruse for working men, and were read chiefly by persons of a higher social grade. Failures pave the way to success. William and Robert Chambers, whose labours in the cause of popular education are so well known and appreciated, had also studied the difficult problem involved in catering for the mental palate of the multitude, and had discerned the causes of the inability of their predecessors in the field to reach the classes which they made their aim. The *Edinburgh Journal*, the first of the popular periodicals, proved a great success, the sale soon exceeding fifty thousand, and nearly doubling during the next ten years.

The Useful Knowledge Society, perceiving the success which had attended the operations of the Chamberses in a field wherein they had reaped only failure, renewed their efforts, and ventured upon the bold experiment of a penny periodical, enlivened with illustrations, far inferior to those which appear in similar publications at the present day, but conveying correct ideas of the places and things represented, and in their day a great source of attractiveness. A large section of the upper class, holding an intermediate position between the opponents and the active promoters of popular enlightenment, saw, or thought they saw, possible dangers to religion and morality if the movement remained under secular direction. Under the auspices of a large and influential body of peers and church dignitaries, the Society for Promoting Christian Knowledge was formed, and entered the new field of publishing enterprise with the *Saturday Magazine*, a periodical which differed from the *Penny Magazine* only in having its title printed in black-letter, instead of roman type, and its contents sprinkled with pious reflections and Biblical references and allusions. Its success did not equal that of the periodicals already in the field, however, and in a few years its publication was discontinued.

The earlier venture of the Useful Knowledge Society survived it, but was eventually driven out of the field by a number of rivals, possessing features of greater permanent attraction, and the appearance of which marked the commencement of a new epoch in the history of periodical literature.

Speculative printers began to reflect that the number of persons who wished to be amused must be very much larger than the number of those who desired to be instructed. They saw *Chambers's Edinburgh Journal* going ahead of its rivals, notwithstanding its higher price, and the absence of illustrations, and, with a keen discernment of the literary taste of the masses, attributed its success to the mild infusion of fiction which its conductors had imparted to it, in the form of short stories of a homely and domestic character, which were even more highly appreciated in the homes of the Scotch peasantry and the artisans of the towns, than by their fellows south of the Tweed. The result of these reflections was the appearance of several broadsheets, differing considerably in character, but all aiming at the amusement rather than the instruction of the classes among whom they were intended to circulate.

One of the earliest of these, if not the first, emanated from the office of John Cleave, a wholesale bookseller and newsagent in Shoe Lane, and one of the six delegates of the working men of Great Britain who, in conjunction with as many Radical members of the House of Commons, drew up the People's Charter, as the document was called, which embodied the views of their constituents on the question of Parliamentary Reform. Cleave, whose shop was one of the chief emporia of the Radical pamphlets of the time, had also played an active part in the dissemination of unstamped newspapers; and in 1837, men of his stamp stood higher in the estimation of the unenfranchised masses than the Whig statesmen by whom they conceived their cause to have been betrayed. *Cleave's Gazette of Variety*, which resembled in form a four-page newspaper of the largest size, started, therefore, with all the advantages derivable from his well-known name, and a title, as fairly as attractively, suggestive of its contents. A roughly-executed political caricature on the first page, and some vigorous writing on the rights and wrongs of the people, recommended the paper to the working men of the metropolis and the large towns of the manufacturing districts, and there was an ample provision of fiction and anecdote for the mental regalement of their wives and the rising generation.

The Penny Satirist differed from Cleave's paper only in containing a larger quantity of political matter, and in reflecting, in that portion of its contents, the views of the Anti-Corn-Law League rather than those of the National Charter Association. It was said, indeed, that it was subsidized by the League, the coarse woodcuts which embellished the front of the paper, and which were graphic arguments for the repeal of the imposts on food, being paid for by the funds of that body, the enormous expenditure of which in the propagation of its principles is well known. This new aspirant to public favour was issued by Cousins, a bookseller in Duke Street, Lincoln's Inn Fields, whose shop, and Hetherington's, in Holywell Street, and Watson's, in Queen's Head Passage, Paternoster Row, were the chief depôts of the literature of unbelief. It never attained so large a circulation as Cleave's paper, however, partly because it had not the recommendation of a name so well known as Cleave's, and partly because the political portion of its contents were less acceptable to the masses who, much as they desired cheap food, thought it of more importance to have the power of preventing the cost of food from being artificially enhanced by legislation.

Both were eclipsed in a few years by another broadsheet, in which politics were eschewed, and the place of the political caricature was taken by as coarsely engraved a representation of some incident of one of the tales and romances which constituted nearly the whole of its contents. This was *Lloyd's*

Penny Sunday Times, issued by an enterprising printer and newsagent, whose business was then carried on in Curtain Road, Shoreditch. The large circulation which this sheet rapidly attained induced the proprietor to issue another penny periodical of the same kind, but without the illustration, and in a form better adapted for binding, namely, that which was subsequently adopted for the *Family Herald*, and since by all the most widely-circulated of the popular periodicals now so numerous. The circulation of *Lloyd's Penny Miscellany* soon equalled that of its predecessor, and Mr. Lloyd was induced by its success, and the piles of manuscripts that were offered him, to issue another and similar publication, with the title of *Lloyd's Penny Atlas*. This, too, was a success, though not of the same degree as the earlier ventures.

The "march of intellect," as it was called, had not then advanced far enough to suggest the possibility, since realized, of its being a remunerative undertaking to engage authors of high literary repute to write for penny publications; but, as in all cases, the existence of a demand creates a supply, authors were soon found who were very willing to write any number of novels and romances for the *honorarium* offered by Mr. Lloyd, that is, ten shillings per weekly instalment of the story. The names of very few of them can now be discovered.

Among them, however, were Thomas Prest, a popular song-writer of that day, and Mrs. Denvil, widow of the tragedian of that name, which will be for ever associated with his unique and inimitable impersonation of Manfred.

Mr. Lloyd was not long alone in a field which enterprising printers and newsagents soon perceived only required judicious cultivation to be profitably worked; and as the publishers of this class of literature multiplied, so did the authors. Among the foremost in the field was Mr. Pierce Egan, son of the author of " Boxiana," and now, and for many years past, editor of the *London Journal*. The stories produced by this popular writer were all of the historical class, and had an immense sale; his earlier productions, " Robin Hood " and " Wat Tyler," having been several times reprinted. Next in the order of popularity comes Mr. Henry Donwes Miles, subsequently editor of a newspaper devoted to " the turf," who, following in the footsteps of Mr. Ainsworth, produced romances embodying the crimes and adventures of Claude Duval, Dick Turpin, and Jerry Abershaw.

Among those who entered this new field of literary enterprise later was the famous Anna Maria Jones, whose " Gipsy Mother " most readers of fiction who are now waning from their prime will remember as one of the favourite novels of their youthful days.

Her "Ruined Cottage" attained a very large circulation. Then there was Stephen Hunt, an occasional reporter, who wrote "Melina the Murderess," founded upon the story of the young woman who shot, in St. James's Park, the soldier by whom she had been seduced and deserted. Later still, there entered the field James Lindridge, a newsagent's assistant, who catered for the appetite which Mr. Ainsworth and Bulwer Lytton had done so much to stimulate, by producing a Newgate romance, entitled "Tyburn Tree."

The demand for serial fiction in this form was still unabated, when the accession of leisure which I derived from the cessation of the Communist propaganda led me to conceive the idea of assisting in the supply. I had written, a few years before, some short stories for a local publication, and I flattered myself both that I understood the requirements of the public taste, and that I could produce a story that would stand out in strong contrast alike t the morbidity and unreality of " Varney the Var " and the sickly sentimentality of " Ada the Betrayed." I did not credit myself with genius, or emulate the fame of the inimitable Dickens; but I had confidence in my possession of a quality which, when combined with a moderate degree of literary ability, is more useful to its possessor, if he does not happen to have been born with a silver spoon in his mouth, than the greatest amount of genius that ever burned, and fretted, and wore its unfortunate possessor into an untimely grave; I mean tact.

I had often, when a boy, gazed upon a set of the series of engravings in which Hogarth portrayed the life of an "unfortunate," and which hung in black frames in the parlour of my maternal grandmother, and tried to understand the story so graphically depicted by the great artist of comedy. The idea which I conceived was to tell this story in type, not, however, adhering strictly to the lines laid down by Hogarth, but introducing characters and incidents not represented by him, in order to illustrate the influence of circumstances in the formation of character. Taking Eugene Sue for my model, I drew upon my personal acquaintance with the actual condition of the lower grades of the people, and the knowledge which I had gleaned of the shadows of London life, for the scenes and incidents which I pressed into my service. Many of them I had actually witnessed, and not a few of the characters were drawn from life.

The conditions amidst which I wrote were not favourable to rose-coloured views of human life and character. The time was winter, always a season of hardship for the poor, and aggravated at that period by legislative enactments devised by Tory rulers for the purpose of artificially enhancing the cost of food for the benefit of the landowners. As in 1842, every form of social evil was rife, and society seemed to be drifting into moral chaos. It was not a time to paint in roseate hues the condition of the poor and the unfortunate, or to smooth down the asperities of life and the jarring contrasts of society. I felt strongly about them, and I wrote strongly.

When I had completed my story, I made a neat little parcel of the manuscript, and proceeded to Salisbury Square, where I presented myself at Mr. Lloyd's counter, and stated my business. I was ushered at once into a room, in which sat a stout gentleman of sleek exterior and urbane manners—not the publisher, I found, but his manager.

"Have you written anything before?" inquired this gentleman, as he opened the parcel, and glanced at the title of my tale.

"Only short stories in a provincial periodical," I replied.

"We are rather chary of undertaking the first productions of young authors," said he, cursorily looking over the manuscript. "We have so many brought to us which are really such trash, that even the machine-boys would not read them, if we were guilty of the folly of printing them."

"You will allow me to leave it, I hope," said I.

"Yes; we will have it read," he returned, "and in

a few weeks you may call again. You see, our publications circulate amongst a class so different in education and social position to the readers of three-volume novels, that we sometimes distrust our own judgment, and place the manuscript in the hands of an illiterate person—a servant or machine-boy, for instance. If they pronounce favourably upon it, we think it will do."

I smiled at this; and though I felt that my story was sensational enough for those who like to be excited or intensely interested by what they read, I asked myself what the housemaid would think of my metaphysics, and whether the machine-boy would appreciate my views of social economy.

I left the manuscript, however, and two or three weeks elapsed without any intimation being received by me of the judgment pronounced upon it by the publisher's strange readers. Then I called attention to it through the post, and was informed, in reply, that the mass of manuscripts on hand had prevented it from being read, but that I should be communicated with again in a week. How anxiously I waited, and how disappointed I was when I learned that it had been pronounced unsuitable, I need not say. There was little consolation in the reflection that it was too good for the readers for whom it was intended, when it was followed by the thought that the editors of half-crown magazines would reject it, if not for its Socialist tendencies, because the author was unknown.

For six months the manuscript lay in a drawer, for there seemed little hope for a story which had been rejected in Salisbury Square. Then I resolved upon another trial, and the next time I was in London I placed it with a newsagent who had made two or three ventures of the kind, which had, however, not been attended with success. At the end of a week he also returned it, but recommended me to try another of the trade, who had formerly been one of the most active of the secret vendors of unstamped newspapers. I acted upon the advice, and the result justified so far the adage that the third time is fortunate.

When the first numbers came into my hands, I was pleased to find that my publisher had got up the work in better form than characterized the Salisbury Square issues, or those of any other house in the same branch of the trade. Ten thousand copies were printed, and they were all sold; and I may add, not in any boastful spirit, but as a ray of light upon the popular literature of that period, that it was twice reprinted—a rare instance of public favour in a branch of literature in which one production was constantly succeeding another. As the story was published anonymously, I had frequent opportunities of learning what was thought of it by those who had read it; but I could never satisfy myself as to the degree in which its success was due to its peculiar tone and tendencies, a point in which I was greatly interested.

In the opinion of those who would have had the working-people of that day devote their evenings to the study of the physical sciences, as well as of those who would fain have restricted the reading of the industrial classes to the Bible and the "Whole Duty of Man," the tales and romances of what I may call the Salisbury Square school were replete with moral contamination; but, trashy as many of them undoubtedly were, there was far less immorality to be found in them than between the yellow covers of the French novels sold in Burlington Arcade; and certainly no more than could, and can, be found in most of the three-volume novels of native origin. They did not, it is true, present such evidences of genius as were found on every page of the works of Lytton Bulwer (the late Lord Lytton) and Mr. Harrison Ainsworth; but the characters and the incidents of the Salisbury Square fictions, compared with those in the three-volume novels and the half-crown magazines, show that the literary tastes of Belgravia and Bethnal Green were at that day very similar. Highwaymen and their mistresses did not figure for the first time in the romances published forty years ago in penny numbers, nor were they presented more attractively in them than in "Rookwood" and "Paul Clifford."

The Salisbury Square fictions may be divided, however, into two classes, one consisting of romances of the kind made popular by Anna Radcliffe, the other of the sentimental novels purveyed to our grandmothers by Anne of Swansea and Anna Maria Jones. The latter predominated in number and popularity, and the cause of the preference for them that was so unmistakably evinced may be discovered by a visit to a minor theatre in an industrial quarter of the metropolis—the Grecian, the Pavilion, or the Surrey, for instance, or (some years ago) the Victoria. It is the domestic drama that draws the largest audiences—the natural portrayal of the character and incidents of real life among the masses that elicits the warmest applause of pit and gallery. We have only to watch the countenances, and listen to the whispered remarks, of the men and women of the lowest grades who crowd the gallery, eagerly gazing and listening, during the representation of a drama that excites their interest by exhibiting the trials of suffering virtue, to be convinced that the appreciation of moral loveliness is as keen, the feeling excited by the contemplation of injustice or cruelty as intense, among the poorest dwellers in Lambeth or Bethnal Green as among the most educated and refined of the residents of Belgravia. The sympathies of even the vicious are invariably enlisted on the side of virtue; and an outburst of honest indignation against the villain of the play, especially if he is a cowardly and treacherous villain, brings together every pair of rough hands to endorse it with applause.

Two of the most successful of the Salisbury Square fictions were "Ada, the Betrayed," and "The Lady in Black," the latter founded upon the well-known story of a young lady who lost her reason through the execution for forgery of her brother, a clerk in the Bank of England, and whose appearance was familiar to many persons who were accustomed to visit or pass that institution forty years ago, when she might frequently be seen walking to and fro before it, a pale, thin figure, invariably dressed in black, waiting for the brother she would never see again. The moral tone of both these stories, and indeed of most of the tales issued by Mr. Lloyd, was unexceptionable, virtue being set in as bright and beautiful contrast to vice as in any of the novels on the shelves of Mudie's library at the present day. It is doubtful, indeed, whether the comparison would not be in favour of the former.

The Salisbury Square school of fiction did a good work in its day. It was the connecting link between the Monmouth Street ballads and "last dying speeches," lives of highwaymen, and terrific legends of diabolism, which constituted the favourite reading of the masses fifty years ago, and the more wholesome and refined literature enjoyed by them at the present day. The literary tastes of a people cannot be formed all at once to a high standard. With the mass, as with each of the individuals composing it, intellectual progress is incompatible with a high standard as the starting-point. As a boy is not likely to read much, if we try to give him a taste for reading by confining him to a set course of Locke and Paley, or even Addison and Steele, so a generation that had but just outgrown the mental aliment provided for it by Fairburn and Bysh, could scarcely be expected to appreciate the novels of Lytton Bulwer, even if they had been within its reach. The way to such appreciation was rightly prepared by the substitution of the Salisbury Square literature for that of Monmouth Street and the Minories.

CHAPTER VII.

THE CHARTIST MOVEMENT.

The little group of Chartists that had existed in my native town in 1842, when their orator, the shoemaker poet, had his famous encounter with Cobden, had long been broken up when the formation of a branch of the National Land Company, founded by Feargus O'Connor to provide the members with small farms by means of co-operation and allotment by ballot, brought the remaining members together again. The result was the re-formation of a branch of the Charter Association; and, as I had become convinced by that time that social ameliorations of every kind must make slow progress until the masses acquired political power, I joined it. The weekly meetings were held at a coffee-house, and at the first of them I was elected a member of the committee, in which capacity I became a member of the general council of the Association.

As I took from that day an active part, and locally a prominent one, in the agitation for the People's

Charter, and the movement has been persistently misrepresented by successive writers, and therefore very imperfectly and erroneously understood, some service will be rendered to the cause of truth, and some material afforded for a chapter of English history which has yet to be written, by a brief relation of the progress of the Chartist movement, from its origin to the time at which my connexion with it commenced.

Properly understood, that movement was a natural and inevitable result of the development of the nation. It had its due and legitimate place in the series of political movements which have been in progress since the twelfth century, and are even yet not completed. A nation never achieves its freedom at a single step. An uprising of the masses may give them the broadest franchises for a time, but the liberty thus obtained is brief and illusory. Englishmen have been engaged for seven centuries in the work of political emancipation; but they have made every step sure, and clenched every nail which they have driven into the coffin of arbitrary and irresponsible power. The landowners first, then the traders, then the workers, with long intervals of fitful agitation between each step, has been the order —the natural and inevitable order—of enfranchisement.

The agitation for manhood suffrage followed

closely, as might have been expected, upon the political emancipation of the shopkeepers. United with the trading classes in the agitation of 1831, the working men were overlooked in the measure of Parliamentary Reform which they had helped to necessitate, and thenceforth had to work alone. The threat of revolution to which the Tories succumbed in 1832 would have been breathed in vain by the middle classes alone; but those classes, having gained their object by the aid of the working men, betrayed their allies, and opposed their enfranchisement with a degree of stubbornness which the upper classes would never have ventured to display.

The working classes, abandoned by their late allies, and opposed equally by Whigs and Tories, formed in 1837 a political organization of their own. The germ of a document soon to be famous was contained in a petition, drawn up by an intelligent working man named Lovett, and adopted by a crowded gathering which took place in that year at the Crown and Anchor Tavern, in the Strand. It set forth the injustice and anomalousness of the existing representative system, which practically excluded the working classes, and, while it limited Parliamentary representation to about one-sixth of the adult male population, gave the election of the majority of the House of Commons to about one-fifth of the electors, through the unequal apportionment of members to constituencies. The remedy proposed was a scheme of Parliamentary reform, embracing manhood suffrage, vote by ballot, annual parliaments, equal electoral districts, the abolition of the property qualification, and the payment of members.

The late John Arthur Roebuck, who was selected by the conveners of the meeting to present this petition to Parliament, advised a conference at the British Hotel in Cockspur Street, to which all the members of the House of Commons who were supposed to be favourable to its objects should be invited. The suggestion was acted upon; but only eight members attended, namely, O'Connell, Roebuck, Hume, Bowring, Leader, Hindley, Thompson, and Sharman Crawford. After two nights' discussion, resolutions pledging them to support the petition were adopted, and were afterwards acceded to by Wakley, Fielden, and Whittle Harvey. The bill in which the "six points" were embodied was then prepared by a committee consisting of O'Connell, Roebuck, Leader, Hindley, Thompson, and Crawford, and six members of the Working Men's Association, namely, Lovett, Hetherington, Cleave, Watson, Vincent, and Moore, and was accepted by the unenfranchised throughout the country as the People's Charter.

Of the twelve authors of that document not one survives. Hetherington, Cleave, and Watson, all booksellers in the metropolis, were known to me from 1841 to 1848, in which year the first-named died. Lovett was a Birmingham man, who wrote a work on Chartism, and was the subject of a sympathetic sonnet by Ebenezer Elliott, the Corn Law Rhymer, which appeared in "Tait's Magazine" in 1840, while the former was undergoing imprisonment for a seditious harangue delivered during the excitement which preluded the conspiracy and insurrection of the preceding year. Vincent was a compositor, and subsequently became known as a popular, and very able and eloquent lecturer, both in this country and the United States.

The movement soon assumed proportions which caused uneasiness to the ruling classes. As the country had been on the verge of revolution in 1831, and the concessions made in the following year included no extension of power to the working men, without whose alliance the threat of revolution would have been made in vain, the danger presented itself again as soon as the industrial classes had organized themselves for single-handed pressure upon Parliament and the Crown. The resistance of the House of Commons to the demand for the People's Charter constituted, indeed, a more serious ground for the fear of revolution than had existed in 1831; for the opposition of the Crown to popular demands could be overcome by the power of the Commons to stop the supplies, and that of the Lords by the power of the Crown to create new peers, so long as the Commons' House was in accord with the people, while an obstructive House of Commons, representing only a small minority of the people, could be overcome only by revolution, or the fear of it.

This became the situation in 1839. The unenfranchised had been organizing for the obtainment of electoral reform—"peaceably if we can, forcibly if we must," as the phrase went amongst them— since the conference of 1837. The House of Commons had refused to concede their demands, and the Chartists, quoting Blackstone's observation concerning taxation without representation, prepared for the alternative so often expressed in their private gatherings.

A convention of delegates from all the branches of the National Charter Association assembled at the Dr. Johnson Tavern, in Bolt Court, Fleet Street, simultaneously with the meeting of Parliament. Their early deliberations were conducted harmoniously; but, as happened again in 1848, the refusal of the House of Commons to even allow the Bill to be introduced caused a rupture, the minority being content to wait until the monopolists of political power should be willing to make concessions, while the majority were resolved to appeal to physical force. The leading members of the majority held private conferences at the Arundel Coffee House, in the Strand; and the advocates of moral suasion, fearing that trouble was brewing, resigned their seats.

Conspicuous among the members of the physical force section were John Taylor, who had been educated for the medical profession, and George Julian Harney, afterwards editor of the organ of Chartism, the *Northern Star*. Taylor had some years previously inherited a fortune of thirty thousand pounds, the greater part of which he expended in the promotion of revolutionary enterprises, first abroad and afterwards at home. During the Greek struggle for independence, he purchased and equipped, at his own expense, a small vessel, with which he joined the insurgents. He was afterwards concerned in a conspiracy of the French Republicans, and was ordered to leave France in forty-eight hours. He was described to me as a vain, impetuous young man, wearing his long black hair parted down the centre, a fashion very generally adopted by advanced reformers a few years later.

Harney was then only nineteen or twenty years of age, as great an enthusiast as Taylor, but a poor orator, as he always remained, though his speeches read well. As I knew him in after-years, he was a pale, delicate-looking man, more intelligent than well educated, and in his manners and conversation quiet and unobtrusive, as I have generally found the most formidable of the conspirators with whom I have been brought into contact to be.

As I was only eighteen years of age at the time when the conspiracy of 1839 burst and collapsed at Newport, and was not connected with the Chartist organization until several years afterwards, the glimpses I obtained of the secret and personal history of the movement were due to individuals with whom I became acquainted at a later period. As I then learned, the threads of the conspiracy were held by the five members of a secret committee sitting in London, who communicated with only one member in each of the branches of the National Charter Association. I have been assured that more than a hundred and twenty thousand men, armed and trained (for drilling had been going on nightly for some time on the moors and hills), could have been placed in the field at an hour's notice; and that there were depôts of ammunition formed at several places in the northern and midland districts.

The late David Urquhart, who claimed to possess an amount of knowledge concerning the conspiracy which I believe no one ever possessed who was not a member of the insurrectionary committee, does not appear, nevertheless, to have exaggerated the extent of its ramifications and the danger with which it menaced the Government. "It was," he says, "a most formidable affair; and far from being the wild, mad business which it is generally supposed to have been. It is calculated that two millions of male adults were either directly engaged or indirectly compromised in it. Its organization, which was marvellously complete, exhibited unmistakable evidence that it was the work of no common intelligence. Compact and coherent in all its parts, like a piece of machinery, with every groove and cog-wheel in perfect working order, it was assuredly the work of no neophyte. To form an effective army out of large bodies of raw recruits, demands, as every one knows, a rare union of military genius, skill, and experience; so also to create a gigantic conspiracy out of the *ruda indigestaque moles* of a discontented population, are required similar qualities—qualities, we may add, more rare, because more refined, than those which are demanded for the construction of an efficient army, and which can only be acquired by a long apprenticeship in the art of conspiracy. Nor in the organization of the Chartist plot were any of these requisites wanting; it possessed, in fact, and that in a remarkable degree, the two great characteristics of a well-constituted secret society, namely, impenetrability from below and perfect perspicuity from above."

The inference drawn by Urquhart was, that the Chartist organization of 1839 was the work of a foreigner, and he traced a resemblance in it to that of the Greek secret association called the Hetairia, in order to found upon their imaginary resemblance the theory that both derived their inspiration from St. Petersburg. The organization of the Hetairia was, however, more than ordinarily complex; while the Chartist organization, according to the sketch given by Urquhart from a paper which he claimed to have seen, and which he alleged was in the handwriting of a member of the insurrectionary committee, was very simple, closely resembling that of the United Irishmen.[1]

I had read Mr. Molesworth's "History of the Period," Gammage's "Narrative of the Chartist Movement," and the "Memoirs and Correspondence of Thomas Slingsby Duncombe," without obtaining any light upon the conspiracy and its authors, when, in 1872, I received a copy of an address delivered at the Cercle Catholique in Paris, by the Abbé Defourny. In turning over the leaves, my attention was attracted by the following extraordinary sentence:—

---

[1] *Vide* "The Secret Societies of the European Revolution." 2 vols. London: Tinsley Brothers.

"England was on the point of becoming the prey of the Commune and the International, then known under the name of the Chartist movement." Of course the reverend orator, knowing nothing about the International—which is merely an European organization of trades' unions—intended by this anachronistic remark, merely to convey the idea that Chartism was synonymous with revolution— the English form of the onward march of nations which Frenchmen of Conservative tendencies describe, as vaguely as comprehensively, as *la Révolution*—as was indeed believed by many persons who had better opportunities of obtaining accurate information upon the subject, but were content to believe what they read in the *Times*, instead of endeavouring to ascertain the truth.

Arrested by the sentence which I have quoted, I read on; and I make no apology for transcribing the following passages, because the number of persons who have read the abbé's address will probably not be one per cent. of the readers of these recollections.

"Not only London, but twenty of the principal towns in England, were about to be laid in ashes by a fire that was only to be quenched in blood. The day and the hour were fixed, and the signal for conflagration and murder was to have been given everywhere at one and the same time. Two days before the day fixed, in the evening, a man appeared, who was endowed with sufficient courage and energy to commit himself with three of the five superior chiefs of the plot—misguided working men, who had not created the conspiracy, but who held in their hands its organization and execution. He spoke to them so forcibly, that he believed he had moved them, but without convincing them. At two o'clock next morning there was a knock at his door. It proceeded from the three men. Had they come to assassinate him, or to renew the conversation? He knew not; but he had the courage to descend alone, and to receive them. After the exchange of a few words, these chiefs of the plot literally fell at his feet, and placed in his hands a list in cipher of the principal members of the conspiracy. He had no sooner deciphered it than he proved to them what he had previously affirmed, namely, that they were unknowingly the instruments of the foreigner against their own country. There were in the list the names of two Russian agents who, a short time before, had played the same game in Greece. The three men at once sent messengers to countermand the order that had been given. There was time. The conspiracy had begun to take effect only in one town, which was situated at a great distance, and there the messenger arrived one hour too late."

But for one circumstance, I should have regarded this story as the result of one of those efforts of the imagination often found in French newspapers, and occasionally in our own. But a gentleman was present when the address was delivered, whom the Abbé Defourny referred to as the individual "who on that day saved his country." That person was David Urquhart, formerly secretary to the British Embassy at Constantinople; and the translation which I have quoted appeared in the *Diplomatic Review*, the property of that gentleman, and the organ of the Foreign Affairs Committees founded by him. As I had gleaned a few details of the secret history of the Chartist movement from some of those political veterans whom Feargus O'Connor called the "Old Guards," I felt curious concerning the revelations made in the Cercle Catholique, and wrote to the editor of the review in which they had been made, asking to be favoured with the names of "the five superior chiefs of the plot," and those of "the principal members of the conspiracy," or at least with the former. To this letter I received no answer; but, six months afterwards, a lengthy article appeared in the same publication, giving further details of the extraordinary incidents related by the Abbé Defourny, combined with an account of the Hetairia and a retrospect of the political condition of the world in general forty years ago.

Beginning with an acknowledgment of my letter, and a random surmise that I was a relative of

John Frost, convicted of treason in 1840, the writer proceeded to state that "the five superior chiefs of the plot" were Major Beniowski, a Polish refugee, well known twenty or thirty years ago as a teacher of mnemonics and the inventor of the logotype system of type-founding; three working men, named respectively Cardo, Warden, and Westropp, and an individual whose name was withheld, but who was said to have held a high position in the police.

I had heard Beniowski mentioned in connexion with the conspiracy thirty years before he was thus denounced by Urquhart. One of the "Old Guards" told me that Beniowski was one of those who were charged with the military organization of the insurrection, but was not one of the authors and directors of the plot, and acted in subordination to the secret revolutionary committee. Urquhart assigns to him the leadership of the revolt in Wales, and to that extent the statement is correct; but it is not easy to reconcile that position with the assertion that he was the head and front of the conspiracy. If he had been, he would either have taken no active part in the movement, or have taken the chief command. He went down to the mining districts of Wales, some time before the outbreak at Newport, to drill the disaffected; but it may be inferred, from a letter written at that time by Dr. Taylor, that the intention of the revolutionary committee to appoint him to the military command there was not abided by. "The Pole," wrote Taylor, "has not gone to Wales, but I understand a much honester man." This also confirms what I was told by others, that Beniowski was not the director of the enterprise, but strictly subordinate to the secret committee.

He had been a member of the Hetairia, and, according to Urquhart, held a high position in that association, to which many other foreigners, English and French political and literary notabilities, as well as Poles and Russians, were affiliated. No evidence was ever adduced by Urquhart in support of his accusation that Beniowski was a secret agent of the Russian Government. If he was, the Cabinet of St. Petersburg, depicted by Urquhart as scattering gold broadcast over the world for the purpose of corruption, was far from liberal towards its emissaries; for he was not a man of luxurious habits, and he died poor. Universal conspirator he certainly was; one of those Poles who, in the words of the national poet, Casimir Brodzinski, "scour the wide earth, invoking liberty;" but, considering how recklessly his denouncer was wont to accuse of being agents of Russia every one who dissented from him, he is entitled to an acquittal of the charge of being an emissary of the Government which has oppressed his compatriots for nearly a century.

I never met Beniowski, nor, so far as I am aware, ever saw him; but I find the following notice of him in a letter written in 1839 by a member of the Convention:—"I have seen Beniowski, and heard him speak, briefly; and I should think him well fitted to exercise influence and acquire authority over men not very capable of thinking for themselves. He was a fine, tall, aristocratic-looking man, and possessed great fluency and no small degree of audacity. He came to us in the latter days of the Convention to ask us to contribute from our funds to assist in the movements of a society, chiefly of foreigners, with which he was connected, but with whom we had no sympathy." This may have been either the Democratic Committee for the Regeneration of Poland, or the Association of Fraternal Democrats.

Cardo was a shoemaker, and Warden a gardener; and both, I have been informed, were men of considerable intellectual powers and attainments. Both, and also Westropp, with whose occupation I am unacquainted, were members of the National Convention; but, I never heard a hint that either of them was a member of the secret revolutionary committee. The only names ever suggested, until Urquhart gave those of Cardo, Warden, and Westropp, were Lowery—mentioned by Gammage in his insufferably dull and uninteresting history of the

Chartist movement, published in 1854, as a man who was supposed to know as much about the affair as anybody—and Bussey, a beer-house keeper at Bradford, concerning whom Feargus O'Connor made the following statement:—

"You remember the ardour, the fervour, the enthusiasm of the representatives of London and Birmingham in the Convention of 1839, and you have not perhaps forgotten the honesty, the courage, the valour of the immortal Peter Bussey, the pompous and mouthing representative of the men of Bradford. This man kept a beer-house, was delegate for Bradford, and devoted his whole time to writing reports of each day's proceedings, in order that his constituents should thoroughly understand the conduct of their representatives. This letter was addressed to his wife, and was not to be read till the factories closed, when the slaves could have an opportunity of receiving the intelligence of their independent representatives. This beer-house was like a theatre; there was a rush for early places, and all paid for admission.

"This fellow got up secret committees, to be held in different parts of the country, to establish the best means for getting up a revolution, of which Feargus O'Connor was to be kept *in utter ignorance*. As soon as the mind was ripened, and when the arm was nerved, two messengers called upon Bussey, informing him that his army was ready for the onslaught. He was lying in bed, pretending to be violently affected with rheumatism, when one of the staunch advocates of Chartism called him a coward, and threatened to shoot him, whereupon the valiant field-marshal, notwithstanding the dire effect of an agonizing pain, jumped out of bed, ran behind a bag of flour, and told them to '*send for Feargus O'Connor,*' although it was to have been kept an utter secret from me.

"Well, upon the following morning, I was at the 'Mosely Arms,' in Manchester, when Richardson, one of the delegates of the Convention, and Aaron, of Bradford, waited upon me, and informed me that the men of Yorkshire were prepared to turn out, and that I should come to Dewsbury and take the command. I told them that I was on my way to London, and that it never was my intention to command troops that I did not marshal myself; however, that I would return to Leeds, and meet any deputation that chose to call upon me. I returned to Leeds by the next coach. Upon the following day, a deputation from Dewsbury waited upon me —a very large deputation—and from whom I anticipated no small share of contention and violence; however, it ended thus: they declared that they had been most atrociously deceived by Bussey and others, and that they would never again place confidence in any leader but the much abused Feargus O'Connor."

I have been informed by gentlemen who were acquainted with David Urquhart, and shared his peculiar opinions, that the list of "the principal members of the conspiracy" included the names of Feargus O'Connor, John Frost, Richard Oastler, and Joseph Rayner Stephens. It happens, however, that the fact of O'Connor's ignorance of the plot does not rest upon his own assertion alone, though that, coupled with the fact that he was not included in the indictment of Frost and others, might be considered sufficient for the conviction of any impartial and unprejudiced mind. Lowery, when questioned on the subject by Gammage, is said to have replied, "Feargus O'Connor knew nothing at all about it; but he was the only man in England who could have prevented it."

Now, if the list contained the name of one man, as a principal member of the conspiracy, who knew nothing at all about it, that is good *prima facie* evidence that it was altogether a spurious concoction. But let us look at some of the other names. Oastler was agent to a Yorkshire landowner named Thornton, and Stephens was a Wesleyan minister. Both were Tories, and their popularity was due to their exertions in furtherance of the movement for limiting the hours of labour in factories. Stephens distinctly repudiated Chartism when on his trial at Chester for sedition in 1840; and two years later he was a prominent supporter of Mr. Walter, then a Tory candidate for the representation of Nottingham. His followers even were not known as Chartists, but were always designated Stephenites.

John Frost was deeply implicated in the conspiracy, and had the chief direction of the movement in his own part of the country. He was the principal draper in Newport, a man of good repute, and one of the Monmouthshire justices until he was deprived of the commission by Lord John Russell on account of the active part which he had taken in the agitation for parliamentary reform. On the day fixed for the outbreak he led a large body of working men, chiefly miners, into Newport, and attacked the Westgate Inn, which was held by a company of infantry hurriedly sent to the spot. The attack failed; and I have been assured that to that failure the collapse of the well-concerted scheme of rebellion was due, as the Birmingham conspirators were awaiting news of success at Newport, the receipt of which would have been the signal for insurrection in all the towns of the midland and northern counties.

There was a lull in the Chartist agitation during the two years following the outbreak at Newport. The organization continued to exist, however, and early in the Parliamentary session of 1842 Sharman Crawford introduced, in a very temperate speech, a motion pledging the House of Commons to take the People's Charter into consideration. The Whigs stood aloof from the discussion, however, and the motion was rejected by two hundred and twenty-six votes against sixty-seven.

There was a split at this time in the popular ranks, and two conventions of delegates were sitting at once, one in London and the other at Birmingham. The former represented the larger section, which adhered to the "six points," and was prepared, if necessary, to appeal to the final argument; the latter, with which Joseph Sturge was identified, represented the smaller section, which aimed at revivifying the union of the middle and working classes that existed in 1831, and to attain that end was prepared to exchange manhood suffrage for "complete" suffrage, whatever that might be construed to mean, and annual for triennial parliaments, which, having regard to the average duration of parliaments, would have been a change scarcely worth contending for.

This division, and the depressing influence of the latter events of 1842, retarded the progress of the movement during the next five years; but in 1847 measures were taken for strong and united pressure upon Parliament in the following session, when a petition for the enactment of the People's Charter was to be presented, bearing a larger number of signatures than had been affixed to any prayer of the people ever laid before the House of Commons.

CHAPTER VIII.

THE GREAT PETITION.

The revival of the Chartist movement in Croydon was inaugurated by a public meeting, held, not at the little dingy public-house in the slums at which Chartist gatherings had previously been held, but in the club-room of one of the principal inns in the High Street; and, as it was announced that three members of Parliament had been invited to attend, we anticipated a crowded meeting. As a precaution against the not improbable non-attendance of those gentlemen, however, we also invited Mr. Macgrath, a member of the Executive Council of the Charter Association; and the event justified it, for neither of the Liberal members we had invited thought proper to attend. The two representatives of East Surrey, Alcock and Locke King, did not even answer our secretary's letter. Peter A. Taylor, who then resided in the town, declined the invitation on the following grounds:—

"An *ill-timed* effort to forward a public question

usually delays, instead of hastening, its accomplishment; and I think there are many reasons why this subject cannot be effectively agitated at present. Had the conduct of many of its friends been more reasonable, I think it might have been the next question to which the energies of Reformers would be directed; but, under present circumstances, I consider this most desirable object will have to be postponed, probably for some years. I regret this upon every account, but must decline to devote time or energy to a subject which, in my opinion, cannot at present be successfully urged."

"Well," said I to my colleagues, "these gentlemen have been invited, and are expected to attend; and their failure to do so concerns nobody but themselves. We shall have as large a gathering as if they were on the platform."

About a quarter of an hour before the time fixed for the commencement of the proceedings, the seven members of the local council left the coffee-house at which their weekly meetings were held, and proceeded to the inn, accompanied by Mr. Macgrath and a reporter from the office of the *Northern Star*. There were not more than twenty men in the room when we entered, but they continued to come in by twos and threes until it was nearly full.

Then we installed as chairman an elderly operative carpenter, named Westoby, who was an old and respectable inhabitant of the town, and went about our work thoroughly in earnest. Macgrath made a very effective speech, and then the first resolution was moved by Hodges, the sawyer—a fine, sturdy example of the best portion of the English working classes—and seconded by myself. While I was speaking the local reporter of the *South-Eastern Gazette*, then the only provincial Liberal journal circulating in Surrey, entered the room, took a few notes while loitering near the door, and then retired, having been present scarcely ten minutes. The resolution condemning the existing representative institutions as anomalous and unjust, and affirming the People's Charter to be the only remedy, was unanimously adopted; and when the petition was laid upon a table near the door at the close of the proceedings, during which the gathering had received a considerable accession of numbers, it was signed by at least three-fourths of those present.

Less than a dozen lines were devoted to this meeting by the *South-Eastern Gazette*, and falsehood and malignity were blended in the reporter's statement that "the chair was taken by Mr. Smallwood, the Socialist;" no such person having taken any part in the proceedings. As only Chartists read the *Northern Star*, in which a full and correct report appeared, everybody else was deprived by this discreditable manœuvre of the means of forming an independent judgment of the great agitation which was then being revived. This was a fair example of the manner in which Chartist meetings were usually reported, whether in the organs of Liberalism or Conservatism.

Hodges was the only member of the local Chartist Council who had been connected with the movement from its commencement, Blackaby having left the town about a year after his encounter with Cobden. I was temporarily residing in London when he left Croydon, and was not aware of his intention; and on my return to the town I found that none of his old associates were acquainted with his new location. It was his habit to disappear in this manner, leaving no clue to his movements; but it was my fortune always to come across him again in some unexpected place.

One evening, in the summer of 1844, I was strolling through the secluded hamlet of Wallington, a few miles from the town, when the sight of an old-fashioned little inn, standing far back from the road, with a smooth green before it, and tables and chairs under the spreading branches of a group of ancient elms, was so suggestive of rest and refreshment, that I was soon seated in the agreeable shade with a glass of ale before me. I was picturing to myself Raleigh and Carew sitting under the venerable oaks of Beddington Park, which formed the background of the landscape, when a man with a small bundle under his arm approached from the dusty road, and, as he came nearer, I recognized Blackaby. The recognition was mutual, and we were both glad to have a chat together, after having lost sight of each other for nearly a year.

He had upon several occasions shown me short poems, the effusions of his imagination; but, unlike most aspirants to poetic fame, he had never had a sufficiently good opinion of his verses to submit them to an editor or publisher, and I had carefully refrained from encouraging him to do so, knowing poetry to be the least profitable ware that an author can carry to the literary market. But to write poetry is a necessity of the poet's existence. Lord Abinger had lately died, and Blackaby had written a poem on the occasion in blank verse, which he thought of printing for private circulation, calculating that he could dispose of as many copies as would defray the cost of its production. He read to me the opening passages, and the address which he had put into the mouth of Satan, as the claimant of the soul of the deceased judge, from which I perceived that the hint for the poem had been furnished by Byron's " Vision of Judgment." There were some passages of considerable literary merit, but the sentiments expressed were calculated to find favour only with those who regarded the subject from the stand-point of the author. It was arranged, however, that it should be printed, and I believe that the fifty copies, to which the order was limited, were all sold.

The evening twilight faded out while we were talking, and I rose to depart. Blackaby followed my example, and we walked a short distance together. The sight of a cactus in a cottage window suggested to him the question whether I had ever seen the night-flowering cereus, the flowers of which unfold their petals at night, and perish before sunrise. He had seen a specimen of this strange and beautiful cactus in the conservatory of Sir Edmund Antrobus, into which he had been admitted by the gardener, and its singularity and beauty had inspired some stanzas, which he produced as he walked, from a well-worn pocket-book. Having obtained his permission to copy them, and to give them publicity if I thought them worthy of the dignity of type, I transferred to my own pocket the sheet of blue-laid foolscap on which they were written, in a hand more bold than elegant, and we parted, the poet retracing his steps towards Cheam, where he then resided.

The poem, which subsequently appeared through my instrumentality in the columns of *Reynolds' Miscellany*, if not a gem of genius, was certainly superior to most of the stuff which is constantly inflicted upon editors, and which they are asked to accept as poetry. But, with the exception of these stanzas and the "Vision," no poem of Blackaby's ever obtained publicity. I afterwards saw others in manuscript, but none of them were equal in merit to these, while the subjects of some of them did not possess the interest required in literary productions intended for general perusal.

Blackaby had made another flitting before the meeting at Croydon, or we might have had the influence of his oratory and argumentative powers to help us. While we were assisting in the preparation of the "monster" petition, the Liberals of France were organizing for a similar movement, led by Odillon-Barrot, and the Republican section was preparing, in the secret societies, to take advantage of the expected collision with the Government. The crash that was impending was seen by me months before it came, for it was clear that the agitation for electoral reform would soon reach a point at which Guizot would have to yield, or adopt such measures of repression as would, as in 1830, bring about the downfall of the Monarchy.

Before the close of 1847 I had declared a revolution in France to be imminent, and expressed my conviction that a vigorous impetus would thereby be given to the agitation for the Charter. The result proved that I was right, though it may be said that it also proved Peter Taylor to be right. Obviously we regarded the matter from different points of view, and could not therefore see it in the same aspect. He foresaw that the House of Commons, representing only a small minority of the nation, would refuse to yield to the representations of the majority, unless the question was taken up by the Government, which was not at all likely; whilst I calculated upon the movement assuming proportions that would command attention from all the estates of the realm, and bind up the cause of the monarchy with that of the people. The movement did assume the proportions that I anticipated, but the Government staked the Crown on the issue of the struggle, and with a success that did not reward the similar position of the Guizot ministry in France.

I was at this time a member of the Association of Fraternal Democrats, meeting monthly at a dingy public-house in Drury Lane, called the White Hart. It was composed of democratic refugees from most parts of Europe, but chiefly of Frenchman, Germans, and Poles, with a sprinkling of such advanced reformers of this country as, like Julian Harney and Ernest Jones, were "Chartists, and something more." Every candidate for admission was required to be proposed by a member, whose nomination had to be backed by another, proposer and seconder being held responsible for the soundness of the aspirant's democratic views, and the correctness of his moral conduct. The motto of the association was "All men are brethren," which was printed on the cards of membership in twelve languages, namely, English, French, and German on the top, above the name of the society, and name and date of admission of the member; in Dutch, Danish, and Swedish on the left; in Spanish, Italian, and Romaic on the right; and in Russian, Polish, and Hungarian on the bottom, below the signatures of the six secretaries, representing as many sections of the society.

I am unable to say whether the association comprised individuals of all the nationalities in whose languages the motto expressing its cosmopolitan character was printed. The democrats of Britain, France, Germany, and Poland were well represented in their respective sections, which, as regards the foreigners at least, formed links of connexion with the secret societies of the Seasons, Young Germany, and Young Poland, the first founded by Martin Bernard in 1839, the others in 1834 by the German and Polish refugees in Switzerland, who, in conjunction with the Italian exiles, formed the association known as Young Europe, under the presidency of Joseph Mazzini.

The Hungarian section was not so strong, there

being comparatively few of that nationality in London at that time; and the Scandinavian section, which embraced the still fewer Swedes, Danes, and Norwegians who held the views of the association, was the weakest of the six. Members belonging to other nations were associated with the sections with which they had the greatest affinity; thus, a couple of Russians were enrolled in the Polish section, obeying the sympathies of community of race, and preserving the dream of the United Sclavonians, consecrated by the blood of Pestel and Mouravieff. There was a Spaniard too, in the French section, who had fought for liberty with Riego and Torrijos. The Italians in London remained outside our organization, most of them being affiliated to Young Italy, and bound by its code not to join any similar association.

I had been received into the Fraternal Democrats on the nomination of Julian Harney, seconded by Henry Ross, a carpenter at Hammersmith. The news of the abdication and flight of Louis Philippe reached this country while we were holding our monthly meeting, and as it had been preceded by intelligence which had caused a considerable degree of excitement among advanced Liberals of all nationalities, there was a very full attendance of members. The tricoloured flag of the French republic; the black, gold, and red symbol of German unity; the green, white, and red tricolour of the Hungarian patriots; the glorious flag that reminded the countrymen of Kosciusko of their lost liberties;—waved with others above the president's chair, and on his right and left sat the secretaries of the sections.

Julian Harney was there, pale and quiet as usual; Michelot, lively, and somewhat excited; Carl Schapper, an artist, whose countenance bore the scar of a wound inflicted by the sabre of a Prussian dragoon; Louis Oborski, a tall, fine-looking man of martial bearing, though far advanced in years, who had borne arms in more than one revolt of his compatriots against the tyrannous rule of the Czar. Below these representatives and advocates of a holy alliance of peoples, sat a mingled assemblage of Englishmen, Frenchmen, Germans, Poles, and Hungarians,—Englishmen who had suffered imprisonment for sedition in times of strong political excitement; Frenchmen who had fought at the barricades with Blanqui and Barbes; Germans who had been expelled from their country for propagating the idea of national unity; Poles who had bled at Ostrolenka; Hungarians who cherished the hope of national independence.

Suddenly the news of the events in Paris was brought in. The effect was electrical. Frenchmen, Germans, Poles, Magyars, sprang to their feet, embraced, shouted, and gesticulated in the wildest enthusiasm. Snatches of oratory were delivered in excited tones, and flags were caught from the walls, to be waved exultingly, amidst cries of *"Hoch! Eljen! Vive la République!"* Then the doors were opened, and the whole assemblage descended to the street, and, with linked arms and colours flying, marched to the meeting-place of the Westminster Chartists, in Dean Street, Soho. There another enthusiastic fraternization took place, and great was the clinking of glasses that night in and around Soho and Leicester Square.

I had few opportunities of attending the gatherings of the Fraternal Democrats; but on this occasion I was in London on business, and I was, I believe, the first person to announce in Croydon the event which I had predicted several months before. Reaching home after the manifestation in Westminster, I hastened to the coffee-house at which the Chartists met, and finding that they had not yet separated, bounded up the stairs, and entered the room in which a dozen working-men were assembled, drinking coffee or lemonade, and reading the *Northern Star* or the *Daily News*.

"Glorious news!" I exclaimed. "Louis Philippe has fled, and the revolution is complete."

"Hurrah!" cried an enthusiastic artisan, inspired by the thought of the influence which the revolution of 1830 had in accelerating the march of parliamentary reform. "Now we shall get our rights."

The excitement created by the revolution in France gave to the Chartist movement the impetus which I had anticipated; but the national petition which Charles Kingsley abused so much in "Alton Locke," without knowing anything about it, had been in course of signature for several months previously. In furtherance of that object, the council of the Croydon branch resolved to convene another public meeting, and, for the two reasons that we anticipated a larger gathering than before, and that two or three of my colleagues, being what are absurdly called "teetotallers," wished to avoid holding it in a public-house, it was resolved to apply for the use of the Town Hall.

There was a doubt, however, as to the authority in whom the control of that building was legally vested, the senior overseer informing me that he did not possess it, and standing aghast at the suggestion of a medical gentleman who came up while we were discussing the question, that the town-crier and bill-poster, being also the head constable under the old parochial system, was the right man to apply to. In this difficulty I acted upon a second suggestion of the doctor, and made an application in writing to Mr. Penfold, a legal gentleman who was at that time clerk to the justices. On the following day Mr. Penfold called upon me, and informed me that the use of the Town Hall could not be granted for the purpose intended.

"What is the objection?" I asked.

"The magistrates," he replied, "feel it to be their duty not to aid or countenance in any way whatever an agitation which they believe would, if successful, be the ruin of the country. There is, of course, no objection to the enfranchisement of a man like yourself; but Parliament could not let in the few who are qualified to exercise the franchise intelligently, and exclude the many who are not so qualified."

"Does not that objection apply quite as strongly to the present state of things?" I inquired. "There is no line of separation now between the ignorant and the educated, the vicious and the virtuous. Every fool or knave who lives in a borough, and pays ten pounds a year rent, has a vote."

"But the objection grows stronger as the qualification is further lowered," returned Mr. Penfold. "I have not time to discuss the question fully, and have called upon you personally, instead of writing, because I am sorry to see you engaged in this mischievous agitation, the success of which you will probably have occasion to regret. Sooner or later these revolutionary movements escape from the control of those who promote them, and the first leaders are rushed over by the mob and left behind."

"I am not afraid of that," I rejoined. "It is only the milk-and-water reformers who are left behind, because they want the courage and earnestness of purpose that are required in the people's leaders, and either fall out on the march, or are cast aside by the men they have fooled and deceived."

Mr. Penfold shook his head, and departed. He failed to see that the Chartist movement, so far from being revolutionary, was strictly constitutional, the ballot being the only one of the "six points" which had not, at one time, been part and parcel of the Constitution. All else that the enactment of the Charter would have done would have merely remedied a defect in the Constitution which was not perceptible in the earlier centuries of its growth; namely, that it did not provide for the admission within its pale of those who, from time to time, might find themselves excluded by the altered conditions of society.

As we could not obtain the Town Hall, and the committee of the Literary Institution were precluded by their rules from granting the use of their lecture-hall for a political meeting, we had no alternative but to hold our gathering in a public-house; and it was held accordingly in the largest room of the Crown Inn, which had always been the head-quarters of the Liberal party when a Parliamentary election took place. It was well attended; and though the Charter Association did not gain any increase of numerical strength from the arguments of the speakers, the extent to which they served the cause was shown by the two thousand and odd signatures which were obtained in the town to the petition.

The treatment of that petition by the House of Commons being a matter of historical fact, this place is as fit as another for recording my testimony that those signatures were all genuine, and for adducing evidence that the fictitious signatures, which were made the excuse for the rejection of the petition, were the work of mischievous idlers and malignant enemies of the popular cause. Macgowan, the printer of the *Northern Star,* said to me one day in his office, when the fictitious signatures were the subject of conversation, "That was the work of idle boys. I heard one of my machine-boys say that he had signed the petition every time he passed a place where it was lying for signature; and 'wasn't it a jolly lark!'"

But the mischief was not wrought entirely by the idle boys of London. In the spring of 1849, when an attempt was made to obtain signatures to a similar petition, I waited upon many of the inhabitants of Croydon for that purpose, and amongst those whom I canvassed was a grocer in the High Street, whose political opinions were unknown to me, as he had been only a few months in the town.

"Oh, I have signed that so often!" he observed, in a careless and half-contemptuous tone.

"Often?" I repeated. "Why, there had not been a petition for the Charter for several years until last year."

"Well, I signed that petition twenty times at least," returned the grocer, with unblushing effrontery. "I used frequently to pass the O'Connor Land Company's offices in High Holborn, and I signed the petition every time I passed."

This confession proves that it was by the enemies of the political enfranchisement of the working classes that the spurious signatures were affixed to the petition—a fact of which Charles Kingsley must be supposed to have been ignorant, but which must be taken cognizance of whenever the history of that period is impartially related.

Every town in England partook of the excitement which was created by the march of revolution on the Continent, and which increased as one success after another was scored by the uprisen nations, and the time drew near for the great popular demonstration which was intended to be held on

Kennington Common on the 10th of April. At the last meeting of the Croydon branch previous to that memorable day, apprehensions were expressed by some of the members that the Government would provoke a collision with the police, and then call out the troops; and the advisability of being prepared for resistance was discussed. I dissuaded those who urged this course from adopting it.

"Let us give no pretext for an attack," I said. "Then, if we are attacked, the Government will have put themselves in the wrong as much as ever Charles I. did, and we can find arms afterwards for a conflict with greater advantages on our side than can be found on Kennington Common."

On the eve of the intended demonstration we learned that Sir Richard Mayne, acting under instructions from Sir George Grey, had issued a proclamation declaring such a gathering to be illegal, and informing all whom it concerned that measures had been taken for its suppression. Close upon this announcement came the private communication that the Executive Council of the Charter Association had resolved to maintain the right of meeting, and proceed with the demonstration at all hazards.

"There will be a fight," observed one of my colleagues, looking grave, and speaking in a thoughtful tone.

"I trust not," said I. "If there must be, it will be a mistake if Kennington Common is made the battle-field. It is on the wrong side of the river."

Notwithstanding the sinister apprehensions of many, my view prevailed with my immediate associates; and I have reason to believe that the vast majority of the tens of thousands who assembled on the following day went unarmed, at the risk of another Peterloo, rather than afford any pretext for a Whig Reign of Terror. I did not know then what preparations had been made by the Government as a precaution against a possible insurrection; but, as I crossed Waterloo Bridge on the morning of the 10th, I saw two lines of police drawn up; and, happening to look over the parapet near Somerset House, I caught a glimpse of a dismounted trooper of the household cavalry, who retired as soon as he found that he was observed. Returning an hour or two later from the offices of the Executive Council, I saw a line of mounted constables, extending from Ludgate Hill to the foot of Blackfriars Bridge, and surmised that they were placed there to close that means of communication, after the working men, who were then swarming over it, were all on the Surrey side of the river.

It was impossible not to feel some degree of

anxiety as to the end, and the feeling increased momentarily in intensity as I proceeded towards Kennington Common, and saw every road converging to that point thronged with working men, pouring in a continuous stream towards the space which had been selected for the intended demonstration. Who could say whether it would be the Government or the directors of the movement whose resolution would falter at the last moment? Who knew whether the tens of thousands who were assembled on the common would refuse to disperse, and the signal be given for a conflict, the consequences of which no one could foresee?

I was standing near the van in which were the members of the Executive Council and many delegates of the National Convention, with the piled-up rolls of the petition, when I heard a cry of "They have got him!" And a wild rush was made towards the western side of the common. Looking in that direction, I saw the giant form of Feargus O'Connor—he and Wakley were the two tallest men in the House—towering above the throng, as he moved towards the road, accompanied by a courageous inspector of police. There was a cry repeated through the vast throng that O'Connor was arrested; a moment of breathless excitement, and then a partial rolling back of the mass of human forms that had suddenly impelled itself towards the road. The tumult subsided; but no one knew as yet what was the situation at that moment.

Presently O'Connor was seen returning, and his reappearance was hailed with a tremendous shout. He mounted the van, and in a few words explained the state of affairs to the anxious throng. He had had an interview with Sir Richard Mayne at the Horns Tavern, and concessions had been made on both sides. The Government had consented to allow the meeting to be held without molestation, and the honourable member for Nottingham had promised to use his influence with the masses for the purpose of inducing them to abandon the intended procession to the House of Commons with the petition. I breathed more freely when I heard this arrangement announced, and I have no doubt that it was a welcome relief to the majority of those assembled from the painful suspense that had been felt while the ultimate intentions of the Government remained unknown.

Mr. T. H. Duncombe states, in his memoirs of his father, idolized for so many years by the working classes as "Honest Tom Duncombe," that the meeting was abandoned—a statement which shows that he knew nothing about the events of that day, and did not take the trouble to inform himself by consulting the *Annual Register*, or the newspapers of the period. It is possible that he may have been misled by a vague recollection that the vast assemblage broke up on the conclusion of O'Connor's speech; but that separation was occasioned by the impossibility of even his stentorian voice reaching those on the borders of the largest assemblage that had ever taken place in England; and it would not, even if the masses had immediately dispersed, have amounted to an abandonment of the meeting. The throng merely separated into three or four bodies, which were addressed by Ernest Jones, Julian Harney, and other popular orators of that stormy period.

Similar misrepresentations have been made, both at the time and since, as to the numbers assembled on that occasion. The lowest estimate of the journals of the following morning was 50,000, which I believe, was as much below the truth as O'Connor's characteristically exaggerated statement in the *Northern Star* was above it. My own estimate was about 150,000, which agreed both with the numbers given by the most impartial of the metropolitan journals, and with the estimate formed independently by Watson, the bookseller, and communicated by him to me shortly afterwards.

The compromise effected at the Horns produced a certain amount of dissatisfaction on both sides. The Chartists would have liked to have carried out their programme to the end, as they had been allowed to do in 1839, when they assembled in Lincoln's Inn Fields, during the sitting of the National Convention, and carried their petition thence in a long procession to the House of Commons. The authorities, on their part, evinced the ill-temper of men who were not accustomed to be thwarted, and had been constrained to make concessions when they would have preferred to enforce their will. The thousands who had crossed the bridges in the morning to congregate on Kennington Common found their return barred by large bodies of police. The cab in which two members of the Executive Council conveyed the petition to the House of Commons was stopped at Westminster Bridge by the police, and obliged to reach New Palace Yard by the circuitous route of Lambeth, Vauxhall, and Millbank.

Blackfriars Road—I was informed by one who traversed it some time after the dispersion of the meeting—was thronged with people, so densely packed that they could scarcely move, owing to the refusal of the police to allow more than two or three at a time to pass through their ranks. Altercations and fights ensued, ending with the more irascible of the crowd being removed in custody, and were followed by rushes at the police, who beat back the crowd with their truncheons.

The exasperation increased as time wore on, and as the crowd became more dense, the pressure upon those in front produced a forward movement which the police were unable to resist. They began to yield ground; the crowd pressed onward, the ranks of the police became broken, and, with a tremendous shout, the dense mass surged over the bridge, sweeping the police before it.

My way lay in the opposite direction. Threading my way through the scattered and scattering groups, I entered the White Swan, on the southern side of the common, to refresh myself with a glass of ale. There, at the crowded bar, stood Blackaby. He had located himself, on leaving Cheam, in Queen Square, Finsbury, where he made gentlemen's boots for a first-class shop in Cheapside, discussed political questions with his fellow-lodgers—the house was full of shoemakers—and wrote verses in his leisure hours. I promised him a call on my next visit to the metropolis, and during the next four years I seldom found myself within a mile of the City side of London Bridge without spending half an hour in the shoemaker-poet's garret.

I remember a sensational incident attending one of my visits which affords a ghastly illustration of the "juxtaposition"—to use a word which he much affected—of life and death in large London houses occupied by working men. I was skipping up the three flights which I had to ascend to reach the garret that served him for both work-room and dormitory, when I was brought up sharp by a black coffin, standing upon the second-floor landing, at right angles to the dirty, uncarpeted stairs. No one stood by the grim and sombre receptacle of poor humanity's mortal remains, the bearers probably resting themselves at the public-house at the corner of the passage by which the little square is entered from Eldon Street. To reach Blackaby's room, I had to step over the coffin, which contained the corpse of a lodger, who had wound up a fortnight's debauch by going home in the still hours of the night and hanging himself.

CHAPTER IX.

THE NEW ORGANIZATION.

The events of the 10th of April have been and are generally referred to as a triumph gained by the supporters of law and order over the promoters of turbulence and anarchy, but nothing can be farther from the truth than that representation. Down to that day there had been no thought of conspiracy or revolt; and, if such had been entertained, it would not have been on Kennington Common that the demonstration would have taken place. It was only when the futility of moral force seemed to be shown by the scorn and ridicule cast upon the most numerously signed petition—not counting fictitious signatures—ever presented to Parliament, and when the minds of the unenfranchised were excited by the preparations made for a conflict, and by the rapidity with which the revolution was sweeping over Europe, that an appeal to arms was thought of.

The first step in that direction was the reorganization of the Chartist body, adopted by the

National Convention, on the motion of Ernest Jones. Until then a subscription of a penny per week, or four shillings annually in advance, had been paid by each member; and the affairs of each branch were managed by a council of five or more members. Under the new organization no subscription was required, and the members were divided into wards and classes, ten men forming a class, and ten classes a ward. The advantage of this plan was that, as was soon to be shown, a large body of men could be called out at very short notice. On the secretary of a branch receiving instructions from the Executive Council, they were communicated by him to the wardsmen, by the wardsmen to the class-leaders, and by the latter to the men of their respective classes. The system closely resembled that introduced by the secret insurrectionary committee of 1839, which was borrowed from that of the United Irishmen—not, as the late David Urquhart laboured to show, from that of the Greek Hetairia, to which it had no similarity whatever.

An ominous change was made at the same time in the composition of the Executive Council, the Convention electing, in the place of the moderate men who had guided the Association in the quiet times of the preceding five years, men who had taken a prominent part in the trials and troubles of 1839 and 1842. Among these was Dr. Macdouall, who had been an active and resolute agitator in those periods, and whose escape from Chester Castle, in which he was imprisoned for sedition in 1840, constitutes an interesting chapter of political romance.

The new organization well stood the test applied to its capabilities on the evening of the 29th of May, when, without any public notification, vast assemblages took place on Clerkenwell Green and Stepney Green, whence processions moved towards the City by routes converging on Smithfield. Uniting on that area, the whole force marched down Snow Hill, along Holborn and Oxford Street, down Regent Street, and through Pall Mall, the Strand, Fleet Street, and Ludgate Hill, into Finsbury Square, where they dispersed. The number of men who marched in that procession was estimated at 80,000. Blackaby, who assisted in the demonstration, told me that he looked back and forward as they tramped along Fleet Street six abreast, and could see neither the head nor the rear of the enormous column, whose sudden and unexpected appearance inspired fear and misgiving both in the City and among the dwellers at the West End.

"Was anything more than a demonstration intended?" I asked Blackaby when, being in London a day or two after the demonstration, I heard his narrative of the affair.

"I believe something was to have been done," he replied, "but I don't know what it was, or why the intention was abandoned. I had no idea of the march until Fussell[1] jumped from the platform and called out, 'Fall in!' Then the men about me began to fall into marching order, and I saw men marshalling them who had white bands round their arms. Some one asked Fussell whether anything was to be done, and I heard him answer, 'I don't know; we shall see.'"

I have reason to believe that Blackaby was mistaken in supposing that "something was to have been done" on that occasion, and that there was no other object in view than a demonstration of force, as a test of the working of the new organization. But there were at that time two bodies directing the movement—namely, the Executive Council and a secret committee; and I am unable to say how far they acted in concert, and to what extent the former were cognizant of the plans of the latter.

"Is it true," I asked, "that arming is going on? We hear a good deal about rifle clubs, and

---

[1] Fussell was said to have been the unknown man who killed the policeman in the Calthorpe Street affray in 1835, when the police attempted to disperse by force a meeting convened in furtherance of the enfranchisement of the working classes. The coroner's jury returned a verdict of justifiable homicide.

life and property protection societies; but what is actually being done?"

"What do you think of this?" said a young Welshman, who worked in the same room, as he produced a pike from a closet. "I can't say much about rifles, but there are hundreds of these in the hands of men who won't hesitate to use them when the time comes."

The pike produced was not the "queen of weapons" eulogized by John Mitchel, the head being roughly finished, and the staff not exceeding five feet in length. Some thousands of these weapons were manufactured in London and Sheffield, but I believe that a large proportion of those fabricated in the capital of Cutlerdom were sent to Ireland for the use of the disaffected in that country.

The rifle clubs and kindred societies which I have mentioned were openly advertised at that time, in the *Northern Star*, as a means of supplying fire-arms to its members, to be paid for by small instalments; and I heard that a Birmingham firm had undertaken to supply any number of muskets at twelve shillings each. The idea of a rifle at that price has been ridiculed by many persons to whom I have since mentioned it; but in 1854 I saw a rifle produced by a Birmingham gun-maker before the Small Arms Committee of the House of Commons, and heard it stated in evidence that thousands of such weapons were supplied to shippers at ten shillings for exportation to Africa. It had brass bands round the barrel, like the Arab muskets, and was not so well finished as an Enfield rifle; but, on the chairman asking whether such a weapon was efficient, the witness replied that it would kill a man as well as a more expensive one.

Communications passed at this time between the plotters of revolution on both sides of St. George's Channel. Macmanus, who was afterwards convicted of treason, and transported to Australia, came to London as an emissary of Young Ireland, and was admitted to a gathering of the Westminster Chartists, at their meeting-place in Dean Street, Soho. By some means a detective contrived also to obtain admission; but he was recognized by some one in the room, and was no sooner denounced than Macmanus ejected him from the room and hustled him down the stairs. On his return journey from London to Liverpool the Irish emissary recognized another detective among his travelling companions; but he contrived to evade the vigilance of the gentleman from Scotland Yard in the neighbourhood of the Liverpool docks, and got safely over to Ireland. His good fortune followed him to Australia, whence he contrived to escape to San Francisco, in which city he lived several years.

Spies and informers, in and out of the police,

were soon busy everywhere. One evening the coachman of a Conservative gentleman came to the room in which the Croydon Chartists met, was enrolled as a member, sat out the proceedings, silent and observant, and—never came again. He had learned nothing, and coffee and lemonade were not the beverages to which he was accustomed. On another occasion a young man of very respectable appearance came to my house and said that he had come from Mitcham, and had been to the coffee-house at which the Chartists met, and, finding that he had come the wrong evening, had been referred to me. He spoke enthusiastically of the revolutionary prospect, and was very desirous of knowing the strength of the organization in Croydon and our preparedness for the expected struggle. I had never seen the man before, and I never saw him again.

The secret committee by which an insurrection was being plotted and prepared for consisted of seven members, named Cuffay, Ritchie, Lacey, Fay, Rose, Mullins, and a man who was known to the others by the name of Johnson, and believed by them to be a working man, but who proved to be a professional pedestrian named Powell, known at low so-called sporting public-houses as the Welsh Novice. Cuffay was a tailor, and was occasionally employed as an accountant at the offices of the National Land Company. Ritchie was a plasterer,

Lacey and Fay shoemakers, Rose a currier, and Mullins a medical student.

Cuffay, who was president of the committee, and appears to have been the concocter of the conspiracy, was an elderly mulatto, of mild demeanour and quiet manners, who worked industriously at his trade, and was apparently one of the least likely men in London to be the leader of a revolutionary conspiracy. He and Rose were the only members of the committee whom I knew, or ever exchanged two words with; and the latter I met for the first time about two months before the conspiracy burst in smoke, without so much as a spark.

Powell, who had joined the conspirators in the hope of making money by betraying them, was as horrible a miscreant as the mind can conceive. Like the wretches who stimulated and then betrayed the Cato Street conspirators, he was constantly suggesting to his colleagues projects of conflagration and slaughter, in order to augment his reward when the time came for him to claim it. It was he who suggested the making of caltrops—pieces of wood, with spikes driven through them—to be scattered in the streets through which cavalry might pass, to lame the horses.

On the 9th of June, being again in London, I called at the office of the Executive Council for the purpose of paying over a small sum of money which had been raised in Croydon as a contribution to the Victim Fund, the object of which was the relief of the wives and children of the Chartists who were then suffering imprisonment for sedition. Among these were Ernest Jones, whose offence consisted in proclaiming to a public meeting that the time would soon come when the green flag would wave over Downing Street; an engraver named Sharp, who died in prison; a baker named Williams, who had been the pioneer of the movement for the sanitary improvement of bakehouses, and the provision of proper dormitories for the employés; and a hawker of fish, whose most seditious utterance was an exhortation that his hearers should not let the Government "brutalize" them—many acts of brutality having been proved against the police, who, in several instances, had fallen upon men as they retired from the meetings frequently held on Clerkenwell Green at that time, and beaten them with their truncheons, such violence resulting in one instance in a fractured skull and the death of the victim.

While I was waiting in an anteroom, I observed a wiry-framed middle-aged man sitting there, with his arms folded, and his head bowed, as if absorbed in thought. As I was about to leave, after being a few minutes with Macrie, one of the Council, I met Dr. Macdouall in the anteroom, and stopped to speak to him. When we parted, the stranger left his seat, and asked me if he had not heard the doctor call me Mr. Frost. In receiving an affirmative reply, he informed me, without the least hesitation, that the preparations for insurrection were completed—arms and ammunition provided, missiles collected on the roofs of houses for assailing the military and police while passing through the streets, and openings made in party-walls to enable the insurgents to pass from house to house. Whit Monday had been fixed for the rising, which was to be prepared for by the massing of the metropolitan branches on Blackheath and Bishop Bonner's Fields.

Those demonstrations had been publicly announced by the Executive Council, and the announcement had been followed by a proclamation from Scotland Yard, prohibiting them on the ground of apprehended danger to peace and order. I felt convinced that the prohibition would be as generally and as resolutely disregarded as it had been on Kennington Common; but I could not feel assured that the night of the 12th of June would pass as quietly as that of the 10th of April had done. What should I do? That question occupied my mind very seriously as the train bore me to Croydon that evening.

Only three days would intervene before the blow would be struck. Arrangements had already been made for a local gathering on Duppas Hill, where, six centuries before, the tournament was held in which the son of Earl Warrenne was slain by misadventure, the occasion being one of the armed gatherings which the barons and knights of the Earl of Leicester's party convened in furtherance of their conspiracy against the Crown. Then the aristocracy plotted and fought against the absolute rule of the monarch; now the masses were combined against the claim of the representatives of a small minority of the people to make laws for, and imposes taxes upon, the unrepresented majority. Was not our movement as natural and as righteous as that of the nobles?

The local portion of the General Council had resolved to convene this meeting several days before I saw Dr. Macdouall, in order to prevent the police of the town from being sent to London on Whit Monday, as they had been on the 10th of April, when the town was entirely denuded of police, and special constables roamed about the streets in the evening, many of them in a state of semi-intoxication, insulting every Chartist or Radical whom they met. In view of the information which I had received in London, our contemplated demonstration assumed an aspect of greater importance.

But what should I do? That question occurred to my mind again and again. The man who had so freely and unreservedly imparted to me the plan of the intended outbreak was a stranger, might be a spy, an *agent provocateur* of the Home Office. On the other hand, he might be a bold man, who knew me by repute sufficiently to feel satisfied that I might be safely entrusted with a secret. That secret I was not going to betray. Clear to my mind as the sun at noon to my material vision was the rightfulness of the meditated revolt. No lapse of time, no legislation of class-elected Parliaments, can deprive a people of the right to reclaim the franchise of which it has been deprived. There can be no Statute of Limitations where a nation's rights are concerned.

No generation of men has the right, even by an unanimous vote, to bind succeeding generations; but there had been no surrender by the British people of their rights, the deprivation against which they vainly protested having been the result partly of usurpation in bygone times, and partly of the growth of social conditions different to those which existed in the infancy of our representative institutions. Therefore, when the majority demanded their rights, and the representatives of the minority, supported by their constituents, met the demand with a stern and peremptory refusal, the excluded masses had, in virtue of the social compact, as clear a right to recover their lost franchises by force as the owner of stolen property has to reclaim it wherever he finds it. I determined, therefore, to impart the information which I received to no one, and thus avoid compromising either my colleagues or myself in the existing doubtful situation. In the meantime, I would guide myself by events as they arose. It would be time enough for us to move when a promising movement had been made in London.

On the night preceding the day that was expected to be so eventful, just as I was about to sit down to supper with my wife, I heard a knock at the door, and, on opening it, saw the stranger who had spoken to me in London at the offices of the Executive Council. Without a word I threw open the door, and he stepped into the hall.

"What has brought you down here?" I inquired, when I had closed the door. "Anything wrong?"

"Nothing that we might not have expected," he replied. "We got a warning yesterday, through Dr. Macdouall, that warrants had been issued at Bow Street for the arrest of a lot of us, and that the Government are resolved to act with vigour this time, and suppress the demonstrations at all hazards. So the intended gathering on Blackheath has been abandoned, and our entire metropolitan strength will be massed on Bishop Bonner's Fields."

"A very wise arrangement," I remarked, with a recollection of the cannon on Westminster Bridge, and the forces stationed on the Middlesex side of all the bridges on the 10th of April.

"The doctor," continued my visitor, "suggested that all who had no special duties in London to-morrow should provide for their safety at once; so I thought I would come down here, and see if I could be of any use."

There is now neither indiscretion nor breach of confidence in divulging the fact that my visitor was a member of the secret revolutionary committee. He slept at my house that night, and on the following morning we surveyed the ground which had been selected for the demonstration. In passing through the town we found considerable excitement prevailing, in consequence of the police having been called in from all the neighbouring villages, and ball cartridges served out to the troops at the barracks. The general impression seemed to be, however, that the magistrates were making "much ado about nothing," and that no disturbance would take place unless the meeting was disturbed by the police.

About noon I received through a policeman a message from Captain Adams, the chairman of the bench, intimating that he would be glad to confer with me at the Town Hall. I put on my hat, and in a few minutes, after elbowing my way through a crowd of policemen and special constables, was in the presence of the justices. Two other members of the Council had been invited, but one of them was absent from home, and the other did not arrive until the conference had closed.

"We have sent for you," said Captain Adams, in his blandest tone, "in the hope that our conference may have the happy effect of preventing such a breach of the peace as we feel assured would be regretted by you equally with ourselves. You are aware that disturbances have arisen elsewhere from the gathering of large assemblages in the open air; and the duty having devolved upon us of taking measures for the maintenance of public order in this town, we have judged it advisable, as prevention is better than cure, to ask your co-operation in that task."

"I have no reason to apprehend any breach of the peace," I rejoined, smiling as I spoke at the oddness of the situation; "but, as a precaution against disorder, we will swear the meeting to keep the peace."

"Why not abandon the meeting altogether?" said the magistrate, persuasively.

"Because," I replied, "in the first place, we believe that we are exercising a constitutional right which we are not disposed to surrender; and, secondly, the abandonment of the meeting, after you have made a display of force, would look very much like cowardice on our part.

"It is only stopping at home this evening," observed the magistrate, with the same persuasive voice and benignant expression of countenance.

"I beg your pardon, sir," said I. "If the promoters of the meeting are absent, many hundreds of their fellow-townsmen will be there, and they will blame us for whatever happens. We have asked them to assemble, and we must be there to meet them."

"Then, sir," said Captain Adams, assuming a grave tone, "I have to inform you that we have received instructions from the Home Office to prevent your meeting, and, in obedience to those instructions, have prepared a sufficient force for the purpose. We shall take possession of the hill, and the police will have orders to arrest you or any other person who may attempt to make a

"Will you have the goodness to inform me under what authority you have taken those measures?" said I.
speech."

"There is our authority!" exclaimed Mr. Sutherland, a stern-looking, dark-complexioned man, who had spent the greater part of his life in India.

He pointed, as he spoke, to a large printed bill which lay upon the table, and which I recognized as the proclamation which had emanated from Scotland Yard.

"I cannot allow to a police ukase the authority of an Act of Parliament," I rejoined.

Mr. Sutherland seemed about to indulge in a violent outburst of rage, but he checked himself; and Captain Adams explained that they were acting under an Act of Parliament passed in the reign of Charles II., which declared illegal all meetings of more than twenty persons.

"Well, you must do your duty, gentlemen," said I, "and I shall do mine; and as I shall have been instrumental in bringing together whatever concourse of people may be on the hill this evening, I consider it will be my duty to be there to meet them."

"Very well," returned Captain Adams. "We are about to adjourn to the workhouse; and if you desire to confer with us again, we shall be glad to see you in the board-room."

Five hundred special constables had been enrolled, and were now sent to the hill on which the meeting was to be held, and which a hundred and fifty soldiers had already occupied. I immediately convened a special meeting of the Council, and informed them of the preparations made to suppress the meeting by force, and of all that had passed between the magistrates and myself. After some discussion a resolution (not of my moving) was adopted, condemning the course taken by the magistrates as arbitrary and unconstitutional; and this I and the mover were deputed to communicate to the magistrates. On sending this into the board-room of the workhouse, we were invited to another conference, the object of which was to elicit from us what had been resolved upon by the Council with regard to the meeting. I replied that we should be guided by the weather (for it was then raining heavily); but that, if the evening was fine, I should be on the hill at seven o'clock, unless the majority decided otherwise.

Until nearly seven o'clock the rain descended in torrents, and then a scout from the hill informed us that the few persons who had appeared were prevented by the police from assembling in groups, and were required to keep moving. The police, horse and foot, numbered eighty, and were the only force visible; the soldiers and special constables being at the workhouse, on the brow of the hill, in readiness to act if required.

The courage of my colleagues was now put to the test. On my rising and asking them what they intended to do, there was a dead silence for a few moments, and then a resolution to abandon the meeting, on the ground of the unfavourable weather and the measures adopted by the authorities, was proposed, and was carried by a majority of, I think, five to two. One object had been attained, however; we had prevented the police and the troops from being sent to London.

"They are at it there now, hammer and tongs," observed Rose; "or," he added, after a pause, "nothing has been done at all."

Scouts from the railway stations brought us no news from the metropolis, and at ten o'clock Rose, who then left us, expressed his fear that the movement had failed. Anxiety weighed heavily upon my mind, however, mingled with a degree of disappointment, as I stepped into the sloppy street; and, leaving the town behind me, ascended an eminence, and looked northward as anxiously as the watchers by the Vistula did on a certain night, half a century ago, when the signal was to be given for the rising in Warsaw. But not one of the conflagrations which Ritchie's corps of "luminaries" were to have kindled reddened the sky.

The troops had by that time returned to the barracks, and at midnight the police were withdrawn from Duppas Hill, the special constables returned to their homes, and Captain Adams telegraphed to Sir George Grey, "All quiet at Croydon." Next day I learned that the troops and police had occupied Bishop Bonner's Fields in numbers which deterred the conspirators from making any attempt at a demonstration. They might have suddenly changed their base of opera

M

tions, and assembled their forces in Smithfield or Lincoln's Inn Fields; but I had afterwards reason to believe that they were not so prepared for a conflict as Rose had represented them to be.

When the crisis had passed, I was so strongly impressed with the conviction that the success of a revolutionary movement was hopeless, owing to the unpreparedness of the conspirators when the time came for the execution of their plot, and the warning which the Government could not fail to take from the abortive movement of the 12th of June, that I resolved to keep aloof from the conspiracy, in which I had not become compromised. I was confirmed in that resolution by a letter which I received from a literary gentleman who had connected himself with the Chartist movement, and was a member of the Fraternal Democrats, advising me not to compromise myself with the revolutionists, and predicting the failure of their enterprise, whenever it might be attempted.

I have reason to believe that Cuffay afterwards became as fully convinced as I was of the hopelessness of the undertaking; but his younger and more reckless colleagues would not hear of its abandonment, and a chivalrous sentiment of honour withheld him from withdrawing from it alone. He went on, therefore, against his own judgment, until at length he found himself in the position of Robert

Emmet on the eve of the abortive movement of the United Irishmen, when it was as dangerous to retreat as to advance.

On the evening of the 15th of August, which was finally fixed for the outbreak, a number of men assembled at a public-house called the Orange Tree, in Orange Street, Bloomsbury, and were in feverish expectation of the signal, when an inspector of police appeared at the door of the room in which they were seated, with a drawn cutlass in his right hand, and a cocked pistol in his left. Behind him those seated opposite the door could see a dozen constables, all similarly armed. There was a movement among the party as he entered, indicative of meditated resistance or escape; but it was checked by the threat to shoot down the first who resisted, or attempted to leave the room.

Commanding each in his turn to stand up, the inspector then searched them, and afterwards the room. A sword was found under the coat of one, and the head of a pike, made to screw into a socket, under that of another. One had a pair of pistols in his pocket, and a fourth was provided with a rusty bayonet, fastened to the end of a stick. Some were without other weapons than shoemakers' knives. A pike, which no one would own, was found under a bench upon which several of the men had been sitting. All of the party were taken into custody, and marched off to the nearest police-station. Ritchie, Lacey, and Fay were arrested in the course of the evening at their respective lodgings.

While these arrests were being made, about 150 men were assembled on the Seven Dials—standing in groups at the street corners, or before the bars of the public-houses. Just after the arrests at the Orange Tree, a man approached a group at the corner of Great St. Andrew Street, and spoke a few hurried words in a low voice to a labourer, who, with a pickaxe in his hand, was directing the attention of his companions to a loose stone in the pavement of the roadway. Almost at the same moment a body of police made their appearance, but apparently without other intention than being in readiness for something.

The man moved quickly from one group to another, and as he left each the men composing it separated, some walking quietly away, and others entering the public-houses at the corner of the streets to communicate what they had heard to those assembled inside. In this manner the number of men assembled on the Dials was reduced in a few minutes to about a tenth of those who had been found there—a result which was attributed by the authorities to the appearance of the police, but was really due to the warning so promptly conveyed to the men.

I have since been informed that the flag of the revolt was to have been first unfurled at this spot, upon which barricades were to have been erected— the beginning of a series to have been extended on every side from that centre—until the insurgents were able to hem in the seat of the Court and the Government. I never heard whose plan this was, and the few hints given me in June were vague and imperfect. Seven Dials was probably selected as the nucleus of the insurrection on account of its contiguity to Whitehall, and the facilities afforded by its narrow streets, radiating in so many directions from a common centre, for a rapid advance.

Cuffay was arrested the next morning at his lodgings, whence he had refused to fly, lest it should be said that he abandoned his associates in the hour of peril. Mullins evaded the search for him for a time, but was eventually discovered, disguised as a woman, at a house in Southwark. Rose escaped. His house in Clare Court, Drury Lane, was searched by the police, and some cartridges and grenades seized, but he had had time to provide for his safety. After being concealed for several weeks at the house of a friend at Somers Town, he ventured to travel to Hull, where he took passage to Hamburg. In that city he obtained employment at his trade, that of a currier, and was joined by his wife and children.

The house in which Powell lived had to be guarded by the police from the time of the arrests until the termination of the trial, and several constables accompanied him to and from the tribunal.

"He deserves death!" Blackaby observed to me one day, during the progress of the trial. "I have a mind to shoot the dog myself."

"You!" I exclaimed, in surprise. "In the street?"

"I," he rejoined; "but not in the street. There would be a better opportunity when he is in the witness-box. He would present a good mark standing there, and in the crowded court I could draw a pistol from my coat-pocket without being observed, and it would be done in a moment."

"Don't think of it," I said. "Conviction is certain, and you would sacrifice your own life without saving the men from their predetermined doom."

"I don't know that my life is worth much," returned Blackaby; "and I have no wife or child to mourn for me."

"Leave the wretch to the fate that is sure to overtake him," I urged. "He will be shunned wherever he goes, for as a spy and informer he will be an outcast from the lowest society in London, and he will end his miserable life as miserably as he has lived—'a broken tool that tyrants cast away.'"

I did not feel sure, however, when I parted from Blackaby that day, that he had abandoned the idea, and I took up the morning paper with an uneasy feeling until the trial came to a conclusion, dreading to learn that the base informer had been carried from the court a blood-stained corpse, and that the poor poet was in Newgate. My persuasion had prevailed however, and Powell was left to the judgment of God.

As I had foreseen, all the accused were convicted. Cuffay, Ritchie, Lacey, and Fay were sentenced to transportation for life, and Mullins to a long term of imprisonment. Powell, who had expected to be handsomely rewarded for his treachery, received only a free passage to Australia. Too idle to work, he found no inducement to remain in that colony, and returned to England a year or two afterwards, a discontented man, believing that he had "saved society," and that society had not adequately testified its gratitude. What eventually became of him I have not been able to discover.

The fate of his fellow spy, the policeman Mullins, is extremely suggestive. Does the reader remember the murder at Hackney of an old woman named Emsley, for the sake of a few pounds which she had in the house, and the base attempt of the murderer to divert suspicion from himself by placing part of the stolen property on the premises of an innocent man? That miscreant was the Home Office spy and informer Mullins, who had been dismissed from the police force for some misconduct, and went on from crime to crime, until he ended his horrible existence upon the scaffold, to which he had so often striven to conduct others.

Blackaby did not live to see the greater part of his political creed made part and parcel of the Constitution on the proposition of a Conservative minister. Failing health induced him to seek the purer air of Northampton, and I never saw him again. Whether he continued to court the Muses, or had all the poetry crushed out of his nature by the severer labour rendered necessary by an inferior description of work, I know not. If he left any manuscripts they have probably been used to light fires, or are stowed away, dusty and cobwebby, in some obscure corner of the house in which he died. His strength diminished as his health failed, and with it the means of supporting life unaided; and he succumbed at last to sickness and poverty, and removed to the house of his brother, in the village of Hunsdon, near Ware, to die.

CHAPTER X.

O'CONNOR AND THE NORTHERN STAR.

My connexion with the Chartist movement as a member of the General Council, and with the National Land Company as a local office-holder, brought me into frequent communication with Feargus O'Connor, and with the men who, as members of the Executive Council, or directors of the company, were most in his confidence. Being acquainted also, with Julian Harney, then editor of the *Northern Star*, and with Ernest Jones, who was on the literary staff of that journal, I had many opportunities of gleaning particulars of the life of Feargus O'Connor, and hearing anecdotes illustrative of his character.

As no biography of that thorough demagogue has ever been published, some particulars of his early life may not be uninteresting, as an introduction to the stories and anecdotes which he was ever ready to tell. It will probably not be a work of supererogation to inform many of the readers of these recollections that he was a younger son of Roger, one of the brothers of Arthur O'Connor, famous as a leader of the United Irishmen, and afterwards a general in the French army. He received his education at various schools in England and Ireland; but, according to his own showing, did little credit to his instructors, being much less disposed to study than to boxing with his fellow-pupils, robbing the neighbouring orchards, and galloping about the country on the horse allowed him by his father. He was expelled from two schools, and the stories he used to tell of his boyish exploits and vagaries leave no room for surprise at the disfavour in which he stood with his father.

After finally leaving school, he and his brother Frank lived with their elder brother Roderick, to whom their father had given a house and 200 acres of land. Considering themselves unfairly treated, both by their father and Roderick, they absconded with two of their brother's horses, with no more definite plan for the future than that of proceeding to England, obtaining employment there, and saving money enough to take a small farm. Having sold the horses at Rathcoole, to obtain funds for their purpose, they proceeded to Dublin, and thence to Holyhead, with the intention of walking to London.

They went first, however, to Bath, where they had an uncle living; but though they remained several days in that city, they could not muster courage enough to call upon him. They walked on, therefore, to Marlborough, where they obtained a week's work at haymaking on a farm belonging to the Marquis of Aylesbury. After a little hesitation as to whether they should emigrate to the United States, or adhere to their original proposition, they resolved upon the latter course, and continued their somewhat circuitous journey towards the metropolis. Reaching Kensington with very little money in their pockets, they stopped at a public-house, where Feargus remained while his brother sought out Sir Francis Burdett, who was an old acquaintance of their father and their uncle Arthur, and Frank's godfather. Burdett had received a letter from their father, who had anticipated that they would seek him, requesting him to send the truants home; and, first exacting a promise from Frank that they would return, he gave him 50*l*. for the expenses of the journey.

Frank was no sooner out of Burdett's house than he regretted having given the promise, and he found Feargus very much disposed to let him return alone. The elder lad, who felt himself bound in honour to return, prevailed upon Feargus to accompany him, however, and they started homeward at once, but with the best disposition to make the journey as long and as agreeable as the ample fund at their disposal would allow. They walked all the way to Bristol, where they embarked on board a sailing packet, and after a stormy passage, during which the vessel lost her mast and rudder, were towed into Cork harbour. In the pleasant capital of Munster they remained a fortnight, "very jolly," Feargus used to say, and still unwilling to perform the *rôle* of prodigal sons. Feargus wished to "cut away again," but Frank said, "I can't break my promise to Burdett." So they started by coach for the paternal mansion, and, after a violent scene with their father, returned to the house of their brother Roderick.

Feargus was afterwards placed in a farm of about 100 acres by Sir Francis Burdett, who also gave or lent him some money for its cultivation. On his next visit to Ireland, Burdett called upon his young friend, who, on his remarking that he saw no stock on the farm, took him to the stable, and showed him a couple of hunters, saying, "There's my stock." Burdett laughed heartily, and gave him a cheque for 150*l*. "And the stock I bought," Feargus used to say, with a jovial chuckle, when he told the story in after years, "was red coats, leather breeches, top-boots, saddles, and bridles."

Farming not being to his taste, he resolved to be

a barrister, as his uncle Arthur had been, and entered himself at King's Inn, Dublin. For this his father disinherited him, as he could not be called to the bar without taking the oath of allegiance, which his father, who was wont to boast of his descent from the mediæval kings of Connaught, regarded as a degradation. Soon finding himself destitute, he borrowed 60*l*. of his brother Roderick, and commenced business as a horse-dealer and trainer, by which, as he used to boast, being a good judge of horses, he cleared in twelve months more than 1000*l*. in excess of his requirements, though "living like a gentleman."

He made his first appearance as a politician in 1822, a period of severe distress in the south of Ireland, when he made his maiden speech in the Romish chapel at Enniskene, in the county of Cork, where a meeting had been convened by himself and the priest. Serious disturbances had occurred at several places, and O'Connor attributed them to the tyranny of the landowners and the Protestant clergy. It was rumoured soon afterwards that he was the secret director of the White Boy insurrection, and as information to that effect was given upon oath, and the charge was never investigated, the story, as it was long afterwards told by himself, may not be uninteresting.

"After his Majesty's loyal troops had gained

the battle of Carriganimme," so runs the story as told by O'Connor, "they advanced upon Deshure, where the White Boys were encamped upon a hill. The Rifles and the Scots Greys arrived at the bottom of the hill before daylight. The side of the hill was covered with furze bushes, high and thick, which afforded concealment to the Rifles; and when, soon after daybreak, the White Boys charged down the hill, knowing that the cavalry could not charge them up the steep incline, there was an awful slaughter when they reached the furze where the Rifles were in ambush. Those who were taken prisoners were tried by a special commission at Cork, and were convicted and hanged.

"Now for my share of the story. Soon after this affair a relation of mine, who was a magistrate, called upon me and advised me to get out of the country as quickly as I could, as Colonel Miller, who commanded the Scots Greys, had informed him that a schoolmaster named Crowley was prepared to swear an information against me, to the effect that I was the generalissimo of the White Boys; that I was with them at Deshure; that I lent them my horses to go out at night to steal arms; and that one of my horses had in one of those marauding expeditions been wounded in the shoulder. Crowley had further stated that when the rebels were routed, and the Scots Greys, contrary to expectation, charged up the hill, I jumped a grey horse over a mud wall that had been erected on the summit as a barricade, snapped a pistol at a captain, and, on its missing fire, took a knife from my pocket, struck the flint, and shot the captain through the arm; also that I wore a blue frock coat, and that a bullet passed through the skirt and wounded me in the leg.

"Well, curiously enough, there was a burnt hole, about the size of a bullet, in the skirt of my coat. I had been smoking a cigar, and some of the ashes had fallen upon it; and, still more curiously, I had a sore leg at the time. So, upon receiving the magistrate's friendly warning, I mounted a horse, rode all the way from Cork to Dublin, embarked with my horse for Holyhead, and rode all the way to London, where I lived thirteen months, until the breeze had blown over, in a humble garret at No. 4, Northumberland Street, in the house of Major O'Flaherty."

O'Connor was little better provided with money at this time than on his first visit to London, and in a short time he found himself obliged to sell his horse. He then turned his thoughts for a time to the possibility of gaining a livelihood by literary pursuits, and with a speed that surpassed the greatest efforts of Scott and James, he produced a novel called "The White Boy," two tragedies, entitled respectively "Constantia and Cardenia" and the "Spanish Princess," a comedy illustrative of Irish life and manners called "Bull or O'Bull," and a farce entitled "Mock Emancipation." He showed them to a gentleman named Adderly, who held an appointment in the Exchequer Seal Office, and who was greatly amused with the farce, but gave him no encouragement to offer either that or his other dramatic productions to a London manager.

He was as destitute of literary ability as any man of ordinary intelligence and education can be, his style being discursive, and his poverty of language, to say nothing of imagination, extreme. Neither the novel nor the plays were ever published; and when, nearly thirty years afterwards, having started a monthly publication called the *Labourer*, of which he and Ernest Jones were the joint editors, he commenced a rambling story called "The Jolly Young Poacher," he soon lost the thread of his plot, and, when it had become hopelessly entangled, left it unfinished.

He was very fond of relating his election reminiscences, and the party-fights and duelling adventures in which he had been engaged in the course of his stormy political career. One of these stories related to Sir John Easthope, who was then proprietor of the *Morning Chronicle*, in which an article had appeared charging him with delusion and hypocrisy. On reading it he went off at once to Sir John's private residence, and not finding him at home, called again and again, at last informing the servant that he would remain until Sir John came in. Presently the baronet arrived, and, on learning the visitor's business, assumed a haughty demeanour, disclaiming responsibility for anything that appeared in the paper, and referring him to the editor.

O'Connor declared that he would hold Sir John responsible, and the baronet finding that his visitor was not easily to be got rid of, and perhaps perceiving that he was not the ruffian that Whig journalists portrayed him, invited him into another room, where his solicitor was awaiting an interview. Sir John then read the article, and expressed his opinion that there was nothing offensive in it, appealing to the solicitor to support that view.

"Let me read the article," said O'Connor; and when he had read it, the solicitor pronounced it offensive; and Sir John Easthope said,—

"Well, I see now from the manner in which Mr. O'Connor reads it that it is offensive, and there shall be an apology in the *Chronicle* to-morrow morning."

On another occasion the *Globe* made an onslaught upon him, on account of a speech which he had made at Bradford, and which, though (strange as it may seem) he usually spoke more temperately than he wrote, was probably somewhat violent in tone.

"When I read it," he said, "I instantly posted off for London; arrived there at seven o'clock in the morning, and went to the *Globe* office at nine. When I arrived, knowing who the editor was, I told him the object of my visit, when he answered that the responsible editor had not arrived, but would be there at ten o'clock. When I called again, I observed a good deal of smirking and smiling, and a man was called to show me up to the editor's room, where I saw a big fellow with enormous moustaches, who, I have no doubt, was hired for the occasion. I read the attack upon me, and told him I had come to demand satisfaction. He asked me in what manner. I replied, by calling the editor out. He was silent for a few moments, during which the fierce expression disappeared from his countenance, and then, after a little discussion of the matter, he assured me that the article should be retracted and an apology made in that evening's impression."

Very amusing, and highly characteristic of the man, were some of his stories of his imprisonment in York Castle in 1839, when he was convicted of sedition and libel, and sentenced to two years' imprisonment. His treatment by the authorities appears, from his own account of it, to have been harsh in the extreme; and, besides being very obnoxious to the Whig Government of the day, his mind was too proud and unbending, his temperament too fiery, to render any mitigation of the unpleasantness of his situation very likely. He was not the man to submit to harsh treatment without protest, and as much resistance as was possible; and for some days after his conviction violent scenes between himself and the governor of the gaol were of constant occurrence. After the third day he was allowed to procure his meals from a neighbouring hotel, and one of his fellow-convicts was allowed to attend upon him daily, and put his cell in order.

He was not allowed to write any articles or letters for publication in newspapers, but he wrote a long narrative of his prison experiences upon the thinnest paper he could procure, with a view to its secret transmission by a very ingenious device. It was the custom in York Castle to allow every prisoner to have a pendant dressing-glass; and when the period of incarceration of the man who acted as his servant expired, O'Connor asked him to bring his glass to the cell. The back was then taken out, the manuscript laid upon the glass, and the back returned to its place. When the man left the prison he received instructions to take the glass to the *Northern Star* office, then at Leeds, where he would receive five pounds. He did so; and O'Connor's narrative was published in the journal under the title of "The Mirror of York Castle."

Some passages of this narrative reflected so strongly upon the conduct of the deputy governor of the castle, whose name was Barber, that upon its publication he went in a rage to O'Connor's cell, and informed him that the magistrates were determined to make a searching inquiry concerning the manner in which he had contrived to send the manuscript to Leeds.

"Very well," said O'Connor, "I am ready for the investigation, and I will let the magistrates know the channel through which it was conveyed. Perhaps you are aware of it?"

"No, I am not," returned Barber, snappishly.

"Don't you remember," said O'Connor, "your bringing me a number of papers, about a fortnight ago, from a debtor, and asking me for my opinion as to the claims of his creditors?"

"Yes, I do," replied Barber, beginning to look thoughtful.

"Do you remember that I returned those papers to you in a sealed cover?" O'Connor asked.

Barber nodded; he felt unable to speak.

"Well," said O'Connor, "all the matter that was sent to Leeds was in that cover, and I am quite prepared for the investigation."

Barber thereupon turned pale, and begged him not to mention the incident of the debtor's papers, as it was contrary to the rules of the prison to do such things, and, if it became known, he would be dismissed from his post. The matter was thereupon allowed to drop.

O'Connor very seldom wrote a "leader" for the journal, his contributions usually taking the form of letters, addressed to the Chartists generally, to those old and tried members of the Association whom he honoured with the distinctive designation of the Old Guard, or to any press or platform opponent whose hostility seemed to call for castigation. His style was vigorous, but coarse, being well sprinkled with expletives, often set forth in capitals, and spiced for the taste of the "fustian jackets" of the Midlands and the North. There was a marked difference, however, between the tone and style of these letters and of those which he addressed to O'Connell in 1836, and afterwards published in pamphlet form, as well as of those in which he related his election contests in Ireland, and which appeared in the *Daily News*. There was the same vigour in the latter, but the absence of the coarseness and scurrility which characterized the former showed that he could adapt his style and his treatment of a subject to the readers whom he addressed.

The fierce invectives and coarse abuse which he

lavished upon his political opponents became more reprehensible as he advanced in years, and with the increased extent to which he indulged in the baneful and degrading habit of intemperance. The strictures of the press upon the National Land Company, and the action of the Government in prohibiting the ballotting arrangement by which its object was to be realized, on the plea that it was a contravention of the statute for the suppression of lotteries, excited him almost to madness. The letters which he published at this time were dictated by him to his nephew and secretary, Roger O'Connor, he pacing the room all the time, with an occasional pause at a table on which a tumbler of strong brandy-and-water stood. In this manner he would dictate a letter to the hostile critics of his land plan, addressing them as "the press-gang," and beginning with "You ruffians!" or to some platform or parliamentary opponent—Mr. Bright, for instance, an epistle to whom he once commenced with "You buttonless blackguard!"

Roger committed to paper every word of his ravings, which appeared in the *Northern Star* just as they came from his lips. There can be no doubt that the mental disorder which, a few years later, necessitated his being placed under restraint in the asylum conducted by Dr. Tuke, had already begun to influence his actions and language, the mental excitement produced by the efforts made to discredit and destroy his small farms project leading to increased alcoholic indulgence, and intemperance aggravating his natural irascibility, and rendering him less able to bear the constant excitement in which he lived. When he left Dr. Tuke's asylum the vigour and elasticity of both mind and body were gone, and the man who had towered, in stature at least, above all his fellow-members of the House of Commons, except Wakley, and been the very type of the "burly demagogue" of the novelist, had become the mere wreck of his former self. He did not long survive this terrible collapse.

The literary staff of the *Northern Star* at the time when O'Connor was dictating these intemperate and vituperative letters comprised Julian Harney, the editor; Ernest Jones, who wrote the second leader, and conducted the correspondence column; and George A. Fleming, who compiled the Parliamentary summary. The direction of the journal was, therefore, in more revolutionary hands than it had ever been before, Harney and Jones being republicans of the reddest type, and members of the Fraternal Democrats, and Fleming a Socialist, who had formerly edited the *New Moral World*. O'Connor held his subordinates with a tight rein, however, which was especially required in the case of the young and enthusiastic Harney, the St. Just of the movement. O'Connor was strictly a constitutional monarchist, and he firmly repressed all tendencies towards a republic, especially *la république démocratique et social*, to which Harney evinced an unmistakable leaning in the latter years of his editorship and of the journal's existence.

Harney came to the front of the movement in 1839, when he was about twenty years of age, by some bold utterances in support of the cause in Smithfield and other places, to which he was prompted by his enthusiasm and his faith in the revolutionary movement which collapsed at Newport. In 1842 he was prosecuted, with O'Connor and the Rev. William Hill (then editor of the *Northern Star*), for conspiracy, by which process he was brought more prominently forward; and, on the removal of the organ of the movement from Leeds to London, he became its editor. He escaped prosecution during the stormy period of 1848, when he and Jones, with Macgrath, who had been a member of the Executive Council, constituted the deputation which conveyed the congratulations of the Chartist body to the Provisional Government of the French Republic, and were received by Ledru-Rollin at the Hôtel de Ville. On the cessation of the *Northern Star* he edited for a time the *Red Republican*, and subsequently the *Democratic Review*, a monthly publication; but both were failures, and he retired from public life, living for several years in Jersey, whence he removed to the United States.

Ernest Jones was educated for the bar, but literature had greater charms for him, as it has had for so many students of Coke and Blackstone; and, his political views bringing him into connexion with O'Connor, he obtained an engagement upon the *Northern Star*, and subsequently the editorship of the *Labourer*. For that magazine he furnished most of the contents—politics, history, fiction, and poetry; but the most stirring of his poetical effusions appeared in the *Northern Star*. His conviction of sedition in 1848 cut short his journalistic career, and when the term of his imprisonment expired the *Northern Star* was declining with the movement of which it was the organ, and, no other literary employment offering, he removed from London to Manchester, and commenced the practice of his profession, in which he continued till his death.

CHAPTER XI.

PAPERS FOR THE PEOPLE.

In looking over some letters on literary matters at the beginning of 1850, when I was sadly in want of occupation, I found a couple from David Page, who was then on the literary staff of William and Robert Chambers, and with whom I had been in correspondence a few months previously. The one of earlier date referred to some literary project of mine which had not been entertained, and is now forgotten, and concluded as follows:—

"As to other literary employment. We are about to enter upon an extensive series of weekly issues of a somewhat higher order than we have hitherto attempted, and for that purpose are anxious to collect a staff of good and efficient contributors. Perhaps you may be inclined to aid us. Our terms will average from twelve to twenty guineas per sheet; say fifteen for ordinary acceptable matter."

The first number of the contemplated issue, the *Papers for the People*, having appeared, I reminded the editor of the promise conveyed in the second letter to communicate with me again when the arrangements were completed; and proposed that I should write a Paper on Utopias, a subject which had never been comprehensively touched. The suggestion found favour with the editor. "The early history of such theories," he wrote, "may be made highly interesting, while more recent schemes ought to be treated fairly and kindly, as emanating from a desire for the public good, however mistaken their authors may have been. I enclose a number as a guide to length and the treatment of the heavier articles. What we especially desire is clearness, conjoined with that breadth and freedom of style which is generally characteristic of the leading reviews."

It was a sensation as novel as it was pleasing to be writing for publishers who paid from twelve to twenty guineas per sheet, and the pleasure was greatly enhanced by the discovery of a bond of sympathy between myself and the editor. The subject of my first contribution was one with which I was familiar, and for the elucidation of which I possessed a considerable store of material, collected during the period of my connexion with the Communists.

The few days that elapsed between the despatch of my manuscript and the receipt of the editor's intimation that it fully met the views and intentions of the publishers, were a period of no little anxiety and suspense. At length the wished-for letter came, and, as I recognized David Page's rather remarkable caligraphy, and eagerly tore open the envelope, there fluttered from between the folds of the letter a cheque for fifteen guineas. The discovery almost took away my breath. When I had fully realized the great fact that I was capacitated, the opportunity being given me, to earn fifteen guineas in little more than half that number of days, I read the editor's letter, which contained a request that I would send a list of subjects likely to be suitable for the Papers, and which I could treat in the same broad and comprehensive manner as I had the Utopias.

The subject selected from half-a-dozen which I suggested for my second Paper was a survey of the secret societies by which the revolutionary movement in Europe had been promoted and guided during the last quarter of the eighteenth century and the first half of the nineteenth. My treatment of this subject proving satisfactory, I was asked to contribute a similar Paper on the secret associations of the Middle Ages, such as the Assassins, the Templars, the Vehmists, and the Rosicrucians. When this had been sent in, I received an intimation from the editor that the year's issue of the

Papers was provided for, and that he could not give me a commission for another for some months, unless some topic of fresh and living interest should suggest itself, the treatment of which would be in my special line.

Both the Papers on the secret societies were written, in fact, before the publication of the one on the social Utopias; which, though I had been careful to express no opinion of my own concerning the societary theories of St. Simon, Fourier, Owen, Cabet, and other ideologists of the age, provoked a considerable amount of unfavourable criticism; not from the reviewers, but from readers of the Papers, who were shocked by the mere mention of such ideas, unless for the purpose of the most severe and unreserved condemnation.

"I enclose for your amusement, I need not say edification," wrote David Page, "a specimen or two of the remarks which the Paper has called forth. I was fully aware that such a topic could not be handled without calling forth animadversions from various quarters, but scarcely expected that the bitterest were to be from our so-called religious friends and supporters. Of course I have acknowledged in a civil way the letters referred to, and merely send them to you as specimens of the inflictions which we have daily and weekly to endure."

As an example of these private critiques, I give a

portion of one of the letters which the editor enclosed to me, premising that the first of two passages specially objected to by the writer was the following, from the first page of the Paper:—" The idea of a state of society free from vice and misery of every description dates from a very remote period. All the ancient nations had a tradition that, in the first ages of the world, man enjoyed an existence uncontaminated by crime and untainted with disease; surrounded by the beauties of nature, and living in innocence and peace upon the spontaneous productions of the earth. Such was the Eden of Moses and Zoroaster, and the golden age of the Greek poets."

"Now I must say," wrote David Page's correspondent, "that though I am not a clergyman, and do not pretend to be at all *strait-laced* in these matters, I was shocked at reading this, so contrary to all one has been taught and believes. Is what Moses wrote only a tradition? Is it not the revealed word of God? 'They have Moses and the Prophets,' our Saviour says. How different is the article I refer to—' Moses and Zoroaster.' I fear that the two sentences considered together forbid the conclusion that it is a mere slip of the pen, and the impression left on my mind is so painful that I cannot forbear from drawing your attention to it. I think that the whole article is objectionable, perhaps negatively objectionable, but that in treating such a subject is surely a great fault. See again the way in which the paper concludes. The Utopian idea is either a recurrence of the same idea in the human mind, or true in principle. The first is negatived; *ergo*, the Utopian idea is correct in principle. I hope that the adoption of the Paper has been hastily done. I should be very sorry to think otherwise, as in my mind it is calculated to do much harm and no good."

I showed this letter to a gentleman of undoubted piety, and whose orthodoxy was equally beyond question. When he had read it, he laid it on the table, with the remark, "What was Eden in the time of Moses but a tradition?" Perhaps my critic supposed that the Israelites preserved no traditions of the early ages of the world, and did not even know that they had grandfathers until the fact was revealed to them in the Pentateuch; but, when all that he advances has been conceded to him, the concession only involves him in the dilemma of having to acknowledge either that the Persians preserved the memory of events which the Israelites had lost, or that the Zend-Avesta was, equally with the books of Moses, the revealed word of God.

The latter sentences of the criticism are a misrepresentation of the sense of the concluding paragraph of the paper, which was as follows:—"The persistency with which the Utopia idea has been reproduced through so many centuries is regarded by some as a proof that the human mind revolves continually in a circle, constantly conceiving the same ideas; and by others as an evidence of the correctness of the principle upon which the idea is based. The progression that has been forbids us to entertain the first belief; and the second involves a problem which will be best solved by posterity. The social ideologies of the present day are, however, evidently the expression of a deeply-felt want, an aspiration after the beautiful and the intellectual, a feeling of sympathy for human woe; and while their authors, and those who adopt them, confine themselves to moral and peaceful means of propagating them, and do not suffer their zeal to mislead them into courses inimical to the continuance of order, we should respect their motives, however erroneous we may deem their opinions. In an age like the present, whatever of good may be contained in the systems that have been passed briefly under review will not be lost; the criticisms of their authors upon present society may be useful in drawing the attention of legislators to many errors and abuses, the dust and cobwebs of the past; and their visions of the future may suggest many modifications applicable to the moral, mental, and material wants of the present generation. We dive for pearls into the depths of the ocean, and descend for gold into the darksome mine; and we should not disdain to search for truths among dreams of Utopia and foreshadowings of the Millennium."

Something like the comments which I have here made upon the kind of criticism of which I have given an example was contained in my next letter to the editor, who responded in the following manner:—"I am much pleased with your note of yesterday, and entirely concur with you, not only in the opinions you have expressed, but in the manner in which you have expressed them. In sending you the remarks of Mr. G. and Mr. W., I did so merely with a view to show you how one's writings are received by certain parties, and because I think it is always well that an author should have an inkling of how he stands with the public. Of course I could have sent you others; for scarcely a number we issue but brings bundles of flattery or of fault-finding."

One word more upon this correspondence. David Page was no sympathizer with Socialism, no Radical, nor (it is to be presumed from the conservatism of his political creed) a sceptic in religion. On the cessation of the papers, he removed from Edinburgh to Cupar, to edit and superintend the publication of the *Fifeshire Journal*, which was his own property, and an exceedingly well-conducted journal, mildly Conservative in its tone and tendencies.

The subjects of my two next contributions to the papers are sufficiently indicated in the following letter:—"I am glad you have grappled with the ancient philosophers. People every day hear of the philosophy of the Hindoos, of Confucius, of Plato, Epicurus, Aristotle, and a dozen others, and yet I don't believe that one in a hundred has a right conception of who these worthies were, and what the opinions and dogmas they propounded. I trust you will produce a first-rate exposition. Very much in the same condition stand the ancient mysteries. Very absurd and superstitious a great many of them may have been, and yet I do not believe them to have been one-half so absurd, superstitious, and wicked as the generality of well-meaning but uninformed Christians regard them. Pray endeavour to set them right on this matter also."

I was very much gratified when my paper on the ancient schools of philosophy was referred to by David Page as "a very admirable *precis* of all that is necessary to be known by the general reader." The paper on the Eleusinian, Isian, and other mysteries of the ancient world, required more study and research than any other subject I had ever written upon. The only existing work on the pagan mysteries was that of St. Croix, and all that I could find in English was the fourth section of the second book of Warburton's "Divine Legation of Moses." But, by wading through an immense amount of ancient history and poetry, I contrived to produce what was, and is, the only work on the subject in the English language, albeit extending only to thirty-two pages.

This was my last contribution to the series, which was carried on with great success for two years, and was only discontinued, as I have been informed, because the publishers desired to make a strong case against the paper duty by attributing its cessation to the operation of that impost. I should not have said so much as I have about my contributions to the papers if their authorship, and that of the whole series, had not been misrepresented in a review the conductors and contributors of which are usually well-informed.[1] On the occasion of the death of Robert Chambers, it was therein stated, as evidence of the literary industry and versatility of the deceased and his brother William, that, besides editing *Chambers's Journal*, they wrote the whole of the *Papers for the People*. As the latter serial was issued weekly, and ranged over every field of literature and science, each paper extending to thirty-two pages, this was making something more

[1] *Athenæum.*

than literary Crichtons of two men whose claim to the grateful remembrance of their generation rests upon their great services to the cause of popular education and enlightenment, rather than upon their literary merits.

They were not even the editors of the periodical with which their name was associated, and which was the pioneer of the popular periodicals of the present day. That was conducted thirty years ago by Mr. Leitch Ritchie. The papers, as I have shown, were edited by David Page, and I have reason to believe that neither William or Robert Chambers wrote a single one of the series. Some of the tales, such as "The White Swallow" and "The Ivory Mine," were written by Mr. Percy St. John; and others, I believe, by Mrs. S. C. Hall. If either of the brothers Chambers wrote any of the papers, I should be more disposed to credit William with the authorship of those on industrial associations and the educational and sanitary movements, and Robert with that of the biographies of Wordsworth, Campbell, and Ebenezer Elliott, than any others of the series; but even of these I am not sure.

CHAPTER XII.

A NEW PHASE OF THE REFORM MOVEMENT.

NEARLY thirty years ago, when I had been absent from my native town about a year, I observed on my return to the neighbourhood signs of a more active and vigorous moral life than my fellow-townsmen had ever been known to exhibit before. Something like an infusion of new vitality had taken place, attributable partly to a considerable influx of population from localities nearer to the metropolis, consequent upon the facilities which the railway afforded for frequent and rapid communication, and partly to the growth to manhood of a new generation. The young men of the middle class, carrying with them the more advanced minds among the middle-aged, were talking of Parliamentary reform, and endeavouring to organize a system of untrammeled discussion.

As I have sometimes been asked for suggestions for the organization and management of working men's institutes, mutual improvement societies, and other associations of a similar character, and as disappointment has often been felt by the promoters of institutions of that kind, when it has been found, after several years' trial, that the class for whose advantage they were devised would not support them, the contribution to the history of the agitation for Parliamentary reform which this chapter contains may be usefully prefaced with a few particulars of the movement referred to at the close of the last paragraph, which may help to solve the problem.

Forty years ago there existed in the town a Literary and Scientific Institution, located in the building which had formerly been the theatre, and in that phase of its existence had witnessed the histrionic triumphs of the Infant Roscius and Miss Foote, afterwards Countess of Harrington. It had, therefore, an excellent lecture-hall, and in addition a good library, the nucleus of a museum, and a spacious reading-room. For several years it was in a flourishing condition, but comparatively few members of the working class were at that time connected with it. In 1843, however, it began to receive a considerable accession of members from the ranks of the workmen and tradesmen's assistants, and a numerously signed memorial was laid before the committee on behalf of those classes, suggesting the formation of a discussion class, and the excision of the rule excluding from the library works on politics and controversial theology, which, it was complained, had been relaxed in favour of works of conservative and orthodox tendencies.

This memorial did not find favour with the committee, which was composed of the local gentry and clergy, who shook their heads at the idea of discussion, and expressed their fear that the young men who had signed it wished "to talk politics." An unfavourable answer was returned, and the influx of artisan members received a check. The middle-class members did not regret this effect, as they objected to the presence of their assistants and workmen in the reading-room; and shortly after the rejection of the working men's memorial their influence procured, under the guise of reducing the amount of the subscription, a system of separate fees for the lectures, the use of books, and the use of the reading-room; so that, while the subscription for the two former objects was somewhat less than had formerly been paid for the three, the several payments were higher in the aggregate than the original single fee. The object of this arrangement was the exclusion of the working men from the reading-room; the effect was to drive them from the institution altogether.

An endeavour to establish a mutual improvement society, on the basis of free inquiry, which was made by myself and a few working men two or three years later, failed from want of funds. A similar cause had, in the meantime, obliged the committee of the institution to discontinue the lectures; many more of the members thereupon withdrew, and, in the end, the building had to be vacated, and the library was removed to a room in the Town Hall, of which each of the half-dozen remaining members had a key.

The lecture-hall had been closed for several years when a knot of intelligent young men, chiefly the clerks and assistants of the principal tradesmen, formed a project for the establishment of a new institution upon a more liberal basis. They commenced operations by convening a meeting in the British school-room, which was literally crowded. A provisional committee was elected by ballot, each person writing seven names upon a slip of paper, which he rolled up, and dropped into a hat carried round for the purpose. There was no nomination of candidates; and, as none of the clergy and gentry had attended, none of their names came out of the hat. Of the names which did come out, the seven which stood highest when the votes were cast up were my own and those of two tradesmen, two tradesmen's sons, a draper's assistant, and a Scripture-reader. Three were members of the Established Church, three were Congregationalists, and one was an undenominational Christian.

Having at our disposal as yet only the school-room in which the preliminary meeting was held, we did not deem it expedient to make any immediate arrangements for lectures; but we determined to have a public discussion in the school-room, hoping that it would attract to us the working men, who as yet held aloof from the institution, waiting to see in what spirit it would be conducted. The subject selected was the influence of steam-driven machinery on the condition of the working classes, and it was arranged that I should open the debate.

The school-room was again crowded, the members of the institution being reinforced by a strong contingent of the men who were as yet waiting and watching. I had a very attentive audience, the subject at that time engaging the attention of the thinking portion of the working classes very deeply, and strongly antagonistic views prevailing. I began with an exposition of the extent to which steam-driven machinery had superseded manual labour, and then proceeded to show that the evil would be recurrent with every new application of machinery, at the same time acknowledging that the severe distress which the change produced was the inevitable consequence of social progress under competitive conditions, and that the results were, on the whole, beneficial to society. From this view I argued that the evils incidental to machinery could be removed only by the workers becoming the owners of the machines, through the agency of co-operative associations, under whose direction machinery would work for them, instead of being an antagonistic power. Some of the speakers expatiated on the beneficial results of machinery, which I had not disputed, and others expressed doubts of the practicability of co-operative production, to which I replied by referring to the success of the Rochdale experiment, the history of which has since been so ably told by Mr. Holyoake.

The discussion brought us such an influx of new members, chiefly of the working class, that we ventured to become tenants of the premises vacated a few years previously by the old institution, and to make arrangements for a popular course of lectures and musical entertainments. These were alternated with discussions on various questions, to which the public were admitted free, and which invariably brought forward a good array of speakers, and contributed very much to the popularity of the institution.

The causes of the failure in the one case, and of success in the other, do not lie very deep. Working men do not like to be treated like children, to have the books they shall read chosen for them; and they naturally resent any attempt to set up barriers between themselves and other classes, when all are associated on the same footing for a common object.

The more active intellectual life of which the new institution was one of the signs was favourable to the growth of a new political agitation, freed from the prejudice which attached to Chartism. In Croydon, as elsewhere, there were many of the middle classes who desired Parliamentary reform quite as much as the working men, though with a different aim; but they wished for what they called a moderate measure, by which they meant one that would enfranchise the shopkeepers of the large unrepresented towns which had been growing into importance during the preceding twenty years, and still exclude the majority of the working men. As the Chartist agitation quietly died out after the excitement of 1848, a new movement was commenced, therefore, and a branch of the Parliamentary Reform Association, which had just been launched into existence under the auspices of Sir Joshua Walmsley and Joseph Hume, was formed among the shopkeepers of the town and neighbourhood, with a sprinkling of other grades of the middle class, such as yeomen, farmers, brewers, &c.

Finding the Chartist organization broken up, and discerning in the new movement a power that might be used with good effect against any Government that took its stand on the finality of the legislation of 1832, I proposed to the Chartists of the locality that we should join it, and endeavour to use its machinery for the furtherance of our own aims. They were at first reluctant to move in that direction, but when the example had been set by Hodges and myself, most of them followed. Their adherence added so considerably to the numerical strength of the local branch of the new association, that I deemed it only fair, as they were nearly all working men, while the majority of the original members were shopkeepers, that they should be represented in the committee. I availed myself of the first opportunity, therefore, to propose the reorganization of the governing body, on the ground that, having been elected when the society was in its infancy, it did not then fairly represent the members, who had increased threefold.

The proposition being carried almost unanimously, we proceeded to a new election, when four members of the ultra section, including myself, were elected; and we could easily have elected one or two more, had we not been afraid of breaking up the movement. The result of the election was the re-election of three tradesmen and two mechanics, and the substitution of three artisans and myself for two yeomen, a farmer, and a brewer.

About the same time, I wrote to the council of

the parent association, offering, for a very moderate salary and travelling expenses, to agitate the question of Parliamentary reforms in the agricultural districts, which had never yet been stirred up about it. Several letters on the subject passed between the secretary, Edward Whitty, and myself, and my proposal seemed for a time to be entertained; but nothing came of it. The funds at the disposal of the council may have been inadequate to the cost of extending their operations; but all that I can confidently affirm is, that the proposition was not adopted.

There may have been another reason. Reformers of the calibre of the gentlemen who directed the Parliamentary Reform Association may have shrunk from the consequences of stirring up an agitation that must have accelerated the realization of the aims of the Chartists. It would have been dangerous to have played over again the game of political tactics which succeeded in 1832. It was always clear to my own mind that every movement for the extension of the franchise must lead eventually to manhood suffrage, with new electoral divisions, so arranged as to give every voter the same amount of political power. The farm-labourers would be the last to be reached by it; but penny newspapers would gradually enlighten their mental darkness concerning politics and political economy, and they would some day share the aims and aspirations of the working men of the large towns.

How the farmers would have stared at the proposition to enfranchise the labourers! They shake their heads at it now, more than a quarter of a century afterwards; but they will see it realized before many years, as they have seen fulfilled my prediction of farm-labourers' unions and strikes, made in the columns of the *Shrewsbury Chronicle* years before the existing unions were formed, or the name of Joseph Arch had been heard.

I was much amused by the look of surprise, which changed the next moment to one of incredulity, with which a Conservative gentleman regarded me when I mentioned the project of a tour through the southern counties for the purpose of stirring up the rural working class on the franchise question.

"I don't think even Walmsley is mad enough for that," he observed, after a pause. "It would not succeed; it ought not to succeed! No, no. What the labourer wants is not a vote, but more pork and bacon; and that he can only get through a reversal of the mischievous policy of Peel."

"How would he get more through their being made dearer?" I asked.

"If the farmers got a better price for their corn they could afford to pay higher wages," he rejoined.

"And that is what must be done. The country will not put up with the present state of things much longer."

"I hear that the country gentlemen are talking of mounting their horses," said I; alluding to a speech that had been made a short time before by a Conservative member of Parliament at an agricultural dinner. "If the Protectionists mean that, and will give me a commission, I will undertake to raise an infantry force, ten times as strong as the cavalry raised among the gentry and the farmers."

He regarded me keenly for a moment, as if seeking to discover whether I was in earnest; then he shook his head, and looked very grave, but he said no more. The Protectionists were in the same position in respect of such a movement as the more violent and less discreet among them were then hinting at, as the slave-owners of the United States were when they raised the flag of secession. They had a great force behind them, which they were afraid to use.

The position occupied in 1852 by the movement initiated by Walmsley and Hume was weakened by a similar cause. What the middle classes most wanted was a diminution of the pressure of taxation, then much greater than at the present day; and if that object could have been gained without Parliamentary reform, they would gladly have refrained from touching that question. But they could not see their way to its accomplishment without an increase of the voting power of the shopkeeping classes; and that involved the difficulty that always stood in the way of their success. They could not bring the pressure from without to bear upon Parliament with sufficient force for the purpose without union with the working classes, and the support of the latter could be obtained on no other terms than the adoption of the principle of manhood suffrage.

When the Council of the Association convened a conference on the question, the members of the Croydon branch elected me as one of their delegates, giving me for a colleague a clothier, named Talbot, a representative of the moderate party. Among the ultra Liberals whom we met in St. Martin's Hall on that occasion were Macgrath and Clark—who had been members of the Chartist executive in 1847—Ernest Jones, George W. M. Reynolds, and Mr. Holyoake; but the representatives of the moderate section constituted the majority. Joseph Hume was voted to the presidential chair, and a debate commenced which extended over two days, and did not terminate without provoking considerable exasperation on the part of the ultras.

It was made evident, at an early stage of the proceedings, that the representatives of the trading or moderate section were much more earnestly intent upon increasing their own power in the House of Commons, for their own purposes, than upon achieving the enfranchisement of the majority. They could not be urged beyond a rate-paying qualification for the franchise, though they knew that the majority of the working classes would be excluded by the operation of the Small Tenements Rating Act, and that in London the majority of the unenfranchised of all classes were lodgers. Hence, the dissensions that arose in the Conference on the second day, and which culminated in Ernest Jones's vehement denunciation of Joseph Hume as a reactionist.

The agitation collapsed shortly afterwards, nor was there any earnest renewal of the struggle for more than a dozen years afterwards, though the question was brought before Parliament on two or three occasions by Mr. Bright and the late Earl Russell.

CHAPTER XIII.

MISSION WORK IN BETHNAL GREEN.

I was acquainted at this time with a young curate, with whom I had some time before made a pedestrian tour through some of the most beautiful portions of the beautiful county of Kent, and who had lately exchanged his first curacy at Haverstock Hill for a similar engagement in the district of St. Philip, Bethnal Green. On the occasion of my first visit to him after this change, our conversation turned upon home missions, and I was led to make some remarks, derived from my own observation, upon the incompetency of many of the scripture-readers, whose mission-fields were the industrial quarters of our large towns, for the accomplishment of the end for which they were appointed.

"They may be tolerably well qualified to deal with the indifferent and the ignorant," I observed; "but they are utterly incompetent to remove the doubts or meet the arguments of the many intelligent men to be found in large towns who reject the Bible as a divine revelation. They may be useful auxiliaries of the clergy in visiting the poor members of a congregation, and tolerably successful in bringing into the fold of the Church the ignorant and the indifferent; but they don't realize my idea of what a Christian missionary in the home field should be in an age like the present."

"There is great difficulty in obtaining men who would," returned the curate. "It is true they are not very highly paid; but many of them, notably those employed by the City Missionary Society, are as well paid as a large proportion of curates, who are drawn from a higher and more educated class."

"The Churches," said I, in continuance of the thought that was in my mind, "send to the ignorant heathen of Africa and Malaysia men qualified by education for the ministry at home, and to the home field of labour they appoint men who can meet the arguments of the sceptic and the unbeliever—it may be the questions of the earnest seeker after truth—only by an ample quotation of texts, which derive all their value from the divine authority claimed for them, and are often inapplicable to the question at issue."

"I have no doubt that a man like yourself would be better qualified for the mission work of a district in which infidelity is rife," the curate observed, after a pause of some moments. "But men like you don't offer, and the societies have, as a rule, to choose between the converted rough and the pious young man whose notions of the right way of spreading the Gospel are derived from the Sunday-school and the Bible-class."

"There is Brown," said I (that was not the name of the man I referred to, but it will do as well as any other). "He said to me the other day that he thought doubt was impious, and that he could understand unbelief only in connexion with moral depravity. What would be the use of such a man endeavouring to convert a honest and intelligent unbeliever, a man who has been earnestly seeking for the truth, but has lost his way?"

"Have you ever thought of devoting yourself to mission work?" my friend asked.

"The idea has crossed my mind," I replied, "but it has not rested in it, for I have never been able to see my way. You know my political creed, and you know that the ideas of nearly the entire body of the clergy are diametrically opposed to it."

"I don't think that difficulty would be insuperable," the curate observed.

Talking over this subject with another friend, who subsequently superintended a home-mission in one of the largest towns in the North, I found myself so warmly encouraged to engage in mission-work that, after some reflection, I made an application for employment to the Church of England Scripture Readers' Association, backing it with the required testimonials.

There had been a little difficulty, and the manner in which it arose may be usefully told as an illustration of the tone and temper of the times. The friend last mentioned, and a gentleman of the medical profession, certified to my thorough respectability and moral fitness; but I was required to produce, in addition, letters from two clergymen of the Church of England, testifying to my fitness for the special duties of a missionary; and it was desirable, though not absolutely necessary, that these should be given by clergymen officiating in the locality in which I resided. With these I deemed myself unlikely to be in very good odour, on account of my Socialist tendencies, and my recent connexion with the Chartist movement; but the incumbent of the district in which I lived had paid me a visit of condolence on the death of my first wife, and his manner had then been most cordial and sympathetic. To him, therefore, I resolved to make my first application.

He received me in a very friendly manner, and I went straight to the object of my visit, observing that the friend who had given me the first testimonial was so well and favourably known to him, that I thought he would not hesitate to endorse his recommendation. After some conversation, he advised me to see the vicar of the parish; intimating, however, that he would give me the required testimonial, in the event of that gentleman declining to do so.

"As I expect he will," said I, as I rose to leave. "The vicar is a Conservative, and he knows me only by name and repute, as having taken a prominent part in the Chartist agitation, and now a member of the Radical section of the Reform Association."

"You still hold the same political views?" said he.

"I have found no reason for changing them," I rejoined.

"Well, I don't know that they should be an objection," said he, reflectively.

Then we parted, and I proceeded to the vicarage. The vicar received me very coldly, and his countenance expressed surprise and perplexity when I acquainted him with the object of my visit.

"I thought you were an unbeliever," he observed.

"You inferred it, perhaps, from my former Socialist associations," I rejoined.

"I know nothing of them," said he; "I rather think that I received the impression from the tendency of something that fell from you at the Institute."

"I remember nothing from which such an inference could be drawn," said I. "There has been no question of a theological character debated there."

"I have been misinformed, then, or you have been misunderstood," said the vicar. "But I have not seen you at church, and—in short, your antecedents are not, in my opinion, in your favour, and I must decline to certify to your fitness for the work you seem disposed to engage in."

"That you have not seen me at church is not remarkable, because I seldom attend your church," I rejoined. "I more frequently attend Christ Church; sometimes St. James's, sometimes St. Peter's."

"That of itself shows unsettled views," remarked the vicar.

"Will you," I asked, "have the goodness to express the grounds of your objection more definitely, so that I may be able to state them correctly to any other clergyman to whom I may apply?"

"To speak plainly," said the vicar, rising as he spoke, as if to intimate that the interview was at an end, "I don't consider a Chartist a fit person to perform the duties of a scripture-reader."

There remained for me only to bow in silence and retire. I returned to the incumbent of St. James's, and acquainted him with what had passed between the vicar and myself. He listened attentively, and smiled when he heard the vicar's final and real objection. Without further hesitation, he gave me a very favourable testimonial, and said at parting, as he offered his hand to me, "I will give you the hand of Christian fellowship, and I sincerely hope that you will succeed."

Having forwarded my testimonials, the second having been given me by my friend the Bethnal Green curate, I went up to Spring Gardens for my first examination in Biblical knowledge, which I had no difficulty in passing. Indeed, there was no question which any person who had ever read the Bible could have had any difficulty in answering.

The district of St. Philip's, Bethnal Green, was then, and had been for a long time, without a scripture-reader, although a grant had been placed by the Church of England Association at the disposal of the incumbent for the purpose of paying one, owing to the extreme wretchedness of the population, which, with the difficulty of procuring decent lodgings, deterred men from undertaking it. This the curate informed me on my calling upon him after my visit to Spring Gardens, and on hearing it, I immediately offered to take the district, in the event of my passing the second examination, of which neither the curate nor myself had any doubt. My friend immediately proposed that we should visit his incumbent, to whom he introduced me, and who, on his part, was pleased with the prospect of obtaining an active and earnest lay assistant, and readily agreed to accept my services in that capacity.

The second examination at Spring Gardens was performed by an austere-looking doctor of divinity, whose countenance reminded me, at the first glance, of Scott's description of the Grand Master of the Templars; but, on a more leisurely survey of his features, as he turned over some papers before addressing me, I failed to discover in them anything "striking and noble." They were more strongly suggestive of the portraits of the sourest Calvinistic preachers of the seventeenth century.

After a few very simple questions, which any Sunday-school child of average capacity ought to be able to answer, he asked me, with a gravity which was very near disturbing my own, "Who built Noah's ark?"

"Noah and his sons," I replied, looking as serious as my interlocutor, though I could scarcely refrain from smiling at the simplicity of the question, which, like those which had preceded it, might have been more appropriately asked by a Sunday-school teacher of a child of nine or ten years.

"Don't you think they must have had some ship-carpenters to help them?" inquired the doctor.

"I have never had my attention directed to that

possibility," I replied. "I limit my answer to Noah and his sons, because, as the ark is the first vessel mentioned in the Bible, there are no Biblical grounds for supposing the existence of ship-carpenters at that period."

"But Noah and his three sons could not have done all the work themselves," persisted my examiner.

"Possibly not," I rejoined. "If there were ship-carpenters at that period, they may have had such help as you suggest; but there is no evidence on that point.

The doctor looked not very well pleased at this rejoinder, and, dropping the subject, asked why Noah's family were saved from the deluge.

"We are not told," I replied. "It is to be presumed, I think, that, if they were less righteous than Noah, they were at least more righteous than those who were condemned, seeing that they were not involved in the general destruction."

"Why do you *presume* so?" asked the doctor, regarding me austerely.

"Because Noah was a pre-eminently righteous man, and also because they did not incur the divine condemnation," I replied.

"There is no evidence that Noah's sons and their wives were more righteous than those who perished," said the doctor.

"May not their righteousness be inferred from

their selection to re-people the earth?" I asked, in as modest a manner as I could assume. "It was them, not Noah and his wife, who were the divinely appointed maintainers of the continuity of the human race."

"No," returned my examiner. "The righteousness of Noah was imputed to them, as the righteousness of Christ is imputed to us."

Before I could follow the doctor, even in thought, through the maze of argument to which this view appeared to lead, he spoke again, informing me, in his most chilling tone, that my knowledge of the Bible was insufficient to justify him in certifying to my competence to perform the duties of a scripture-reader. I rose immediately, bowed silently, and left the office.

I proceeded immediately to the lodging of my friend, the Bethnal Green curate, and thence to the residence of the incumbent of the district. Both gentlemen heard my report of my examination with surprise, and expressed the opinion that I had come through the ordeal with credit, and that both my logic and my theology were better than those of the reverend doctor.

"I am sorry," said the elder clergyman, "as much for the poor people of my district as for you."

My rejection was a matter of little consequence to

myself, but I felt annoyed by it, and suspected that the reason which had been assigned for it was not the real one. Was it possible, I asked myself, as the train bore me homeward, that I had been rejected for no other reason than because I had hesitated to assume the existence of ship-carpenters before ships, and doubted the examiner's assertion that the all-wise God had chosen to re-people the earth with men and women as corrupt and wicked as those whose abominable vices had prompted Him to sweep them from its face? Was the prominent part which I had taken, locally, in the agitation for Parliamentary reform, and the refusal of the vicar on that ground to certify my capacity for mission work, known to the examiner, or to the committee of the association? I could not answer these questions, and they troubled me much, not on my own account, but as they affected the interests of true religion.

In the evening I visited the friend who was subsequently superintendent of the Leeds mission, and told the story of my failure over again, with the comments thereon of the Bethnal Green incumbent and his curate.

"Your rejection does not say much for the society's zeal for the salvation of souls," he observed, with more warmth of feeling than he was in the habit of displaying. "It looks as if they would rather leave one of the most neglected districts in London in its present condition of spiritual destitution than appoint a man for its relief who cannot subscribe to the crotchets of their examiner."

"Or who regards justice between man and man as an inseparable portion of the Gospel," I added. "Is there any political reason at the bottom, do you think?"

"It is not improbable," he rejoined.

"That is what I cannot understand," said I, expressing a mental difficulty which did not then present itself for the first time. "The men who provide the funds from which scripture-readers are paid, and who express the greatest regard for the welfare of the working classes, as a rule, oppose every effort of those classes to obtain their political enfranchisement, and give their support to that system of 'one law for the rich, and another for the poor,' which is the natural result of class legislation. Why, then, do they support scripture-reading associations?"

He looked grave, supported his head upon one hand, and did not immediately reply. The question seemed to be troubling his mind as it had mine.

"In order that the poor may be taught contentment, so that the rich may live in peace," he at length replied.

"Then their reading of the Gospel is not mine," I rejoined.

No comment upon my friend's answer is now needed. The change of ground effected in 1867 by the former upholders of the monopoly of political power by a small minority of the nation, whether that change was due to conviction of the justice or of the expediency of the enfranchisement of the majority, has, happily for society, left no ground for the painful contrasts of former times.

One of my clerical friends having given me a letter of introduction to the then rector of Whitechapel, the Rev. W. W. Champneys, I had an interview with that estimable clergyman, who expressed the warmest sympathy with my aim and interest in its accomplishment. I cannot now recollect whether it was at his or some other well-wisher's suggestion that I waited upon Mr. Geldart, the secretary of the Towns Mission Society, who placed my name upon the list of candidates for employment. Having answered that gentleman's questions satisfactorily, I presented myself, on an appointed day, for examination by the committee, who, it seemed, enjoyed that business too much to delegate it to a secretary.

The ordeal which I went through upon this occasion was very different from my examination at Spring Gardens, and not nearly so amusing. No endeavour was made to ascertain the extent of my

Biblical knowledge, or even the orthodoxy of my views of the Christian faith, the process adopted being one of moral dissection, in which the principal wielder of the scalpel was a gentleman with a red and bloated face, watery eyes, and large sensual mouth. This gentleman seemed very anxious to elicit from me a confession of the kind made by the converted thieves and costermongers who are from time to time introduced to the public, and greatly disappointed when he found that I had no revelations of vice and blackguardism to make.

Of course he did not express in that manner the grounds of the opinion he formed, that I was not quite the sort of man they had hoped for; but that is the way in which it presented itself to my mind. His brother committeemen intimated their concurrence in his judgment, and there remained nothing more to be said. I shook the dust off my feet as I stepped into Red Lion Square, and troubled scripture-reading organizations no more.

As I removed to London about this time, in the autumn of 1853, and my temporary abode was in Stepney, I occupied my leisure in amateur mission work among the wretched iuhabitants of squalid and poverty-stricken Bethnal Green, and assisting the curate of St. Philip's in teaching the ragged urchins who attended his Sunday-school. The condition in which I found the mass of the population of that district pained and depressed me more than any other revelation of the social depths of our large towns that had ever come upon me. Nowhere else had I ever seen poverty of the same extent or the same degree as that in which the toilers of Bethnal Green were at that time sunk. It was not the poverty which a large proportion of the working class everywhere becomes acquainted with at one time or another, but hopeless, helpless, chronic destitution, which crushes the sufferer down to a little more than vegetative existence most painful to contemplate.

I no longer wondered, after a few perambulations of the lanes and courts of the Friars' Mount district, at the paucity of the attendance at St. Philip's church, and the listless faces of the pale worshippers whom I met there. This was one of the several churches which had been erected a few years previously with funds supplied in response to an appeal to the Christian public, setting forth the spiritual destitution of that quarter of the metropolis; and the average attendance was about one-fifth of the number for whom seats had been provided. With the exception of the church in Victoria Street, Westminster, designed to relieve the spiritual destitution of Strutton Ground, I never sat in a place of worship in which the worshippers were so few in proportion to the accommodation.

The causes of this almost general neglect of the outward observances of religion were not to be found on the surface. The curate could only tell me that the people did not come to church; and that needed no telling. The majority of those who did attend were women, most of them poorly clad, the few desperate attempts that were made to conceal the poverty of the wardrobe being too transparent to escape attention, and too painful to excite a smile. In what proportions the few listless worshippers represented the shopkeepers and the working class I could not learn, all classes alike being steeped in poverty to the eyes.

The result of my inquiries, and such observations as I could make, showed that the paucity of worshippers was not due either to unbelief or dissent, both of which indicate more exercise of the intellect than is compatible with such a low material condition as then prevailed among the masses of Bethnal Green, whose minds were engrossed almost constantly with the one thought—how to get the next meal, to replace some worn-out garment, or to pay the rent of the one miserable room in which, as a rule, each family lived and slept. Wide-spread heathen ignorance, which there were no agencies for reaching—indifference on the part of many, soul-crushing misery on the part of more—those were the chief causes of the almost empty churches of Bethnal Green thirty years ago.

CHAPTER XIV.

JOHN CASSELL AND HIS LITERARY STAFF.

SHORTLY after I had settled myself in London I was introduced to the late John Cassell, whose name was at that time "familiar in the mouth as household words." It met the eye at every turn; on every dead wall and hoarding; in the advertisement pages of every publication. Though it may be doubted whether it would ever have been known—except by such brief and circumscribed fame as may be won by not very brilliant oratory in the advocacy of total abstinence from alcoholic beverages—if he had not been favoured in no ordinary degree by fortune, he was, in some respects, a remarkable man. Born at Manchester in 1817, in a lowly position, he was entirely self-educated, and had worked for years as a carpenter before he set out upon that lecturing tour in the provinces which was his first introduction to public life. The earnestness which he evinced in the cause with which he thus became honourably associated won him a wife and a fortune.

His connexion with the total abstinence movement was a good foundation for the establishment of an extensive business in tea and coffee, and his warehouse in Fenchurch Street, under the able management of Mr. Smith, soon became as famous as his publishing emporium in Belle Sauvage Yard. John Cassell's teas and coffees were advertised in the boldest type, on the cover of every magazine, in the columns of every newspaper, in immense posters, that everywhere met the eye, in conjunction with *Cassell's Family Paper* and *Cassell's Popular Educator*. Both publications had an extensive circulation, and the value of the latter in the promotion of self-education among the masses has been acknowledged in public by more than one of our leading statesmen. The *Family Paper*, which was the older periodical of the two, addressed a far larger portion of the reading public than the other, however, and had a proportionately larger circulation.

The *Family Paper* was a judicious combination of the pictorial newspaper with the popular periodical, containing a serial story and a chronicle of current history, the latter illustrated with portraits, historical scenes, and views of places to which a temporary interest was given by the events of the time. The Russo-Turkish campaign in the valley of the Danube, and the struggle in which our own countrymen and the French were engaged with the army of the Czar in the Crimea, were illustrated by the pencil as well as described with the pen, and, as the illustrations were printed from electrotypes procured from the office of *L'Illustration*, they were equal to those which embellished the illustrated newspapers published at six times the price. The serial stories were furnished by Mr. Percy St. John and Mrs. Burbury, and the historical narrative, with much of the other matter, by the editor.

Cassell's Magazine of Art had not so large a sale as either of the other serials issued with the same prefix, and from the same office, though it was ably edited, printed on fine paper, illustrated as well as any similar publication in existence, and numbered among its contributors the Howitts and their daughter, Miss Meteyard, (better known at that time by her *nom de plume* of Silverpen), the late James Hain Friswell, Mr. J. E. Ritchie, Mr. Dallas, and Mr. E. B. Neill, whose "London Gossip" was then, and for many years afterwards, the most distinctive feature of the *Albion*, and the favourite Liverpoolian reading. The illustrations were, with few exceptions, of Parisian origin, electrotypes being obtained from the celebrated *imprimerie* of Best et Cie. of all such subjects in the publications therefrom issued as were suitable for the purpose, and which were thus reproduced with all the beauty and fidelity of the originals.

I had some conversation with Cassell, on the occasion of our first meeting, concerning the popular periodicals of that day, and, on learning that I was one of the authors of the *Papers for the People*, he thought that I could be useful to him in the conducting of his own serial publications. Early in the following spring I received a letter from him, asking me to call at his office at my earliest convenience; and on the following morning, just as ten o'clock was booming over the City, I passed under the archway of Belle Sauvage Yard, which at that time presented a very different aspect to that which it has assumed since the erection of the present extensive premises of his successors.

On the left, just through the archway, which in the old coaching days was the entrance to the courtyard of the ancient inn from which the place derives its name, there was a dingy and dilapidated building, the greater part of which was propped up within and without, to prevent the whole from crumbling and cracking, until it came down with a crash. This was the printing-office. Farther up, on the same side of the yard, but detached from the main building, was a six-roomed house, the ground-floor of which was used as store-rooms, the apartments above being occupied by the proprietor and the gentlemen composing his editorial staff.

In a sparely furnished room on the first-floor I found John Cassell, a tall sallow-complexioned man, with straight black hair, and a pleasant expression of countenance. He was generally to be found there from eleven to four, smoking a cigar, with which indulgence he solaced himself for his abstinence from wine and beer. When I entered the room he was sitting at a table strewn with letters and newspapers, smoking as he read; but he rose on my entrance, and, there being only one chair in the room, leaned against the table, still smoking.

An understanding is soon arrived at between two persons when, as in this instance, both have the art of conveying their ideas in a few words, and perceive that it will conduce to their mutual advantage. Professor Wallace had resigned the editorship of the *Popular Educator*, and it had been arranged that Mr. Millard, who had hitherto conducted the *Magazine of Art*, should have the responsible direction of both publications, receiving assistance on the latter from a sub-editor, who was also to translate Charles Blanc's magnificent work on the old masters for another serial, " The Works of Eminent Masters," which had hitherto been done by Mr. Percy St. John. This sub-editorship was offered to me, and as it promised useful and congenial occupation, I accepted it.

I had been very pleasantly employed there for about a fortnight, when the door of my room was opened one morning, and, the sound of strange footsteps causing me to look up from the proof I was reading, I saw a fair-haired feminine-looking little man hobbling towards me—a pleasant-looking dwarf, with crooked and shrunken legs.

"Good morning," said he, in a soft and agreeable voice that harmonized well with the feminine aspect and expression of his countenance. "I have come to ask a favour."

"I hope I shall be able to grant it," returned I, very favourably impressed by the little man's pleasant face and manner. "What can I do for you?"

"I want an article on the war for the *Family Paper*," he replied. "I have been absent from the office more than a fortnight through illness, and I find myself rather pressed for matter this week."

"I shall be happy to assist you," I responded.

"You know the sort of thing we want," he continued. "The popular clap-trap about British valour, and a compliment to the Emperor, you know. It has all been said before, but we must say something about recent events, for our war illustrations are exceedingly popular, and that is the key that our accompaniments must be played in."

"You have condoned the 2nd of December, then?" I observed, with a smile, remembering that Napoleon III. had been vigorously attacked at that period in the *Family Paper*.

"He is our ally and very good friend now," he rejoined. "You will let me have the article to-day? Thanks."

He was pursuing his tortuous course towards the door, when he remembered something else, and came back to my table.

"Mr. Cassell wished me to ask you," he said, "whether you could undertake the correspondence column of the *Paper*. You have seen Green, that sour-looking old man, who looks as if he had had a fight with the world, and got the worst of it, and now resented his defeat upon all mankind? He makes the indexes, and extracts from works, and does the correspondence column; but he performs that part of his duty in such a sour and cynical manner, often answering a correspondent with a sneer or a rude rebuff, that Mr. Cassell would like to have it done by some one else."

"I think I can manage it," said I, and the little man then retired.

That was John Tillotson, the editor of the *Family Paper*, and one of the most amiable men whom I have come in contact with in the whole course of my varied life. I was in daily intercourse with him for several months, and saw him occasionally after our paths in life separated, and always found him the same gentle and pleasant associate, notwithstanding his delicate health and temperament. He had a very happy and genial style of writing stories for boys, several of which were published by Griffith and Farran, in St. Paul's Churchyard; and his industry enabled him, besides editing the *Family Paper*, and writing much of the matter, to produce several works of that description, and to write leaders and London letters for a couple of provincial newspapers.

On the following morning a boy brought me a handful of letters from readers of the *Family Paper* in all parts of Great Britain, containing questions upon a great variety of subjects. I have met with persons who believe that the correspondents of periodicals are the creations of the editors. The letters which I found every morning upon my table would have convinced them of their mistake; though, as I pretend to no skill in graphiology, and did not act as a matrimonial agent, my correspondents were not so numerous as those of the publications which devote two or three columns of small type every week to judgments upon the handwriting, or the colour of the hair of their readers, give advice as to the choice of lovers, and put young men in quest of wives in communication with young women in want of husbands. Green resented the transfer of this portion of his duties to me very seriously; and, as I had no reason for desiring it, it was not long before he was allowed to resume it. The old gentleman seemed to think that I had been instrumental in temporarily depriving him of his occupation, for he behaved very grumpishly to me ever afterwards, and ultimately took his revenge for the imaginary injury in a very characteristic manner.

I had a very pleasant time for six months. Mr. Millard was often absent for a day or two, finding he could work better at home; and contributors to the magazine who then called came into my room, as well as at other times, when, having seen him, and not being too busy, they came in for a chat. The Howitts I never saw, and Miss Meteyard was not a frequent contributor; but Friswell and St. John came in occasionally, and their conversation afforded an agreeable relief to the daily grind of translation, varied only by the manufacture of "padding."

James Hain Friswell I remember as a pleasant, though rather dandified young man, with a profusion of very light and very curly hair. He did not impress me at that time, either by his conversation or his contributions, with the idea that he would ever attain a high reputation. His most remarkable production of that period was a brief note which I received from him in the spring of 1855, when he was conducting a periodical which combined some of the features of a newspaper with those of a literary publication, somewhat after the manner of the magazines of the last century. That it was a failure scarcely needs to be recorded. As I had at that time opportunities of occasionally gleaning political information of an important character, I offered him the benefit of them, and was equally surprised and amused when I found his intimation that "exclusive intelligence would be acceptable, and be remunerated at a moderate rate," followed by the qualification that it "must be condensed into a line and a half." I did not inquire what would be the moderate remuneration for that quantity of matter.

I have said that Miss Meteyard was not a frequent contributor, but she was the first whom I had the pleasure of meeting. I had been on the staff only a few days, when Mr. Millard rushed one morning into my room pale and excited.

"Here is Miss Meteyard coming up with some complaint!" he exclaimed. "Some mistake—I can't explain now; but pray see her, and say I am not here."

In a moment he had disappeared into his own room, the door of which he closed and locked; and, before I had recovered from my surprise, the overseer ushered into my room a fair-haired young lady, who was evidently suffering from mental excitement. I rose to receive her, and the overseer, who had sent one of the reading-boys to warn Mr. Millard of her coming, explained the object of her visit.

"Miss Meteyard complains of an error in the composition of her last article," said he. "I have explained to her that it was a mistake of the compositor, which was unfortunately overlooked by the reader, but she wishes to see Mr. Millard."

"Mr. Millard is not here at present," said I, turning to the lady, and placing my only chair for her, "but I shall be happy to be the medium of anything you may wish to say to him."

"Such a very stupid mistake is unpardonable!" exclaimed Miss Meteyard, her tone and manner evincing strong excitement. "Mr. Millard should have detected it, and had it corrected. Look at that, sir!"

Producing the last number of the magazine, she pointed to a line in an article from her own pen, in which Adonais had been printed Adonis, in a quotation of the first line of Shelley's monody on the death of Keats.

"Oh, weep for Adonais—he is dead!"

"It is so ridiculous," she continued. "It makes nonsense of the quotation. Adonis was a youth beloved by Venus."

"I sincerely sympathize with you," said I, "and I am sure Mr. Millard will regret extremely a mistake so annoying to you; but what can we do, beyond making a note for an *erratum?*"

"It is so vexing! I could cry about it," returned the fair authoress, and I feared for a moment that she would do so; but, having relieved her mind by the statement of her grievance, she calmed under the influence of sympathy, and presently took her departure.

"What is the matter?" inquired Mr. Millard, re-entering the room, after opening his door softly, and looking towards the stairs to assure himself that his unwelcome visitor was gone.

In a few words I acquainted him with the cause of our lady contributor's excitement.

"It is my fault," said he, looking rather foolish. "I struck out the *a* myself in the proof, supposing it to be an error of the compositor. But who ever heard of Adonais?"

"Shelley applies the name to Keats," I returned. "It looks like Greek."

"I never read a line of Shelley in my life," said he.

Towards the close of 1854 Cassell came into my room one afternoon, and, standing with his back to the fire, with the invariable cigar between his lips, informed me that he had become involved in pecuniary difficulties which obliged him to discontinue the least remunerative of his publications, and to dispense in consequence with the services of Mr. Millard and myself. A few days after I vacated the sub-editorial stool, I called at the office to see Tillotson. While we were talking of the uncertain future prepared for by this change, Green came in, and, having heard a portion of our conversation, informed me, with his sourest look, that at a place in the Strand, which he mentioned, several poor men were wanted to hawk books. Poor old fellow! I hope he enjoyed his joke as much as I did.

CHAPTER XV.

PROVINCIAL JOURNALISM AND JOURNALISTS.

The number of newspapers published in the United Kingdom had increased so much since the repeal of the stamp duty that I felt encouraged, on the termination of my Belle Sauvage Yard engagement, to aspire to the position of a journalist. Penny newspapers had become possible for the first time, and Reuter's telegrams placed them, in respect of foreign news, upon the level of the old and higher-priced papers. Surely, I thought, there must now be three newspaper proprietors competing for the services of one editor or leading article writer, instead of three journalists competing for every vacancy.

I had contributed some letters on Parliamentary reform to a provincial journal, and others on Owen's home colonies and the small farm plan of O'Connor, in two of the most widely-circulated London newspapers, in 1847; and during the two following years I had been an occasional contributor to the columns of the *Northern Star*. O'Connor had commended my letters on his project in his paper, and I had no diffidence as to my ability to exercise the profession of journalist with credit to myself and advantage to the cause of progress.

I did not know then how little effect the abolition of the stamp had had in promoting the interests of journalism. The truth was, however, that the advantages of the fiscal change were confined, so far as journalists were concerned, to the multiplication, in a small degree, of daily papers. The great number of new provincial journals that sprang into existence in 1853 not only did not increase the demand for journalists, but unfavourably affected the interests of the profession by diminishing the circulation of the previously existing papers, and thus obliging the proprietors to reduce their literary staff or to employ writers of inferior ability.

The new journals may, with a few exceptions, be divided into three well-defined classes. There are, first, those which were started for the purpose of supplying a cheap vehicle for local intelligence, and which realize the ideas of Cobden on the subject by giving a sheet of news and advertisements, without articles, long or short, on the public questions of the day, political or social. Another class consists of papers one side of which is printed in London, and contains the general news of the week, with or without a London letter and editorial matter; and the other, containing local news and advertisements, in the town in which the paper is published. The third class comprises journals of entirely local production, and containing editorial matter, provided in most cases by the proprietor, and generally as brief in quantity as it is poor in quality. In most instances, the staff of a paper of this class is limited to one young man, who acts as reporter and reader, and is expected to "fill up his time at case," which reduces him to the level of the compositors, except that he receives a few shillings per week more, or about three-fourths of the wages of a bricklayer.

For example, I received a letter in the year 1855 from the proprietor of a newspaper issued in a small town in a south midland county, inviting me to a preliminary conference with him at a tavern in the city. I kept the appointment with the punctuality which is one of my acknowledged qualities, and had waited *solus* in the parlour until I had begun to consider whether I should have another glass of ale or leave, when there entered a stout, red-faced man, of the type to be encountered at every step at the Agricultural Hall during the cattle-show week, and who, in his broad-rimmed hat and top-boots, might have sat to Leech for the many portraits of John Bull with which he enlivened the pages of *Punch*.

"Are you the young man who advertised for an

editorship?" he inquired, looking at me steadfastly.

I answered affirmatively, and, having rang the bell and ordered a pint of ale, he sat down. Some remarks of the kind strangers thus situated are apt to exchange when an interval has to be filled up were all that were ventured upon until the ale was brought, and he had filled and lighted a long clay pipe. Thus primed, he entered upon the business which had brought us together. He was the proprietor, editor, printer, and publisher of a moderately Liberal paper, and he required the assistance of a young man capable of sub-editing, reporting, and reading. There was a nice little cottage in the neighbourhood, which he thought would just suit me, and he had no doubt that I should suit him, and that we should get on very comfortably together. And now, what wages did I expect?

"Two pounds," I replied, that amount, be it observed, being the then ordinary remuneration of a printer's reader in London offices, and less than was paid in news offices.

"Two pounds a week!" he repeated, opening his eyes to their utmost capacity; "why, I give my overseer only five-and-twenty shillings."

"What was your expectation on the subject?" I asked as gravely as possible.

"I couldn't give anything like that money," he rejoined, shaking his head.

"Then I must beg to decline your offer, and wish you good morning," said I, rising.

The old gentleman returned my salutation somewhat gruffly, and in another moment he was alone with his pipe and his pint.

It was my good fortune to obtain, shortly afterwards, an engagement as leader-writer and London reporter on a first-class Birmingham journal, the organ of the advanced Liberalism of the district. Understanding that there was a growing demand for thoughtful writing on such matters as co-operative societies, industrial investments, workmen's dwellings, trades unions, and the like, I took these for my earlier subjects, and soon had the satisfaction of knowing that my treatment of them was appreciated. I do not, however, claim for them brilliance of style as the cause of my success, which I am disposed to attribute to their being separated by a broad line from the newspaper articles on the same or similar topics, which were written by gentleman who, knowing nothing about such questions, treated them in the vein of Josiah Bounderly, of Coketown.

I was soon called upon to deal with political questions, and it was a matter of much self-gratulation to me that my journalistic career commenced at the time when the steadily continued demand for Parliamentary reform had at length impressed Lord John Russell with the conviction that the legislation of 1832 upon that question could not be final. That he should have maintained the contrary for twenty years is a fact which shows more tenderness for his party than knowledge of the people or respect for the Constitution. If the Act of 1832 was to be final, it should have provided for a more extensive redistribution of seats, and a wider extension of the franchise in boroughs; and it should have been passed without the Chandos clause, which gave the county franchise to the fifty pound householders. That Tory device, more cunning than clever, was the thin end of the wedge which every successive dealing with Parliamentary reform has driven farther into the Constitution. It was the first step towards the assimilation of the county and borough franchises, and the constitution of new electoral districts on the plan proposed by the People's Charter. If the old lines of the Constitution were to be preserved, every town should have been made a Parliamentary borough, as in the time of Edward I., and the franchise should have been extended to every male adult living in a borough, but restricted to freeholders in the rural districts.

The sweeping away of the distinction between county and borough franchises would, however, have been a measure worthy of a great statesman, who would not have hesitated at an innovation if he saw that its adoption would conduce to the welfare of the nation. Unfortunately, the Whig leader was only a well-meaning, but not very far-sighted, political tinker; and the Reform Bill of 1854 was the worst that was ever laid before Parliament. It proposed nothing for the removal of anomalies which struck at the root of the principle of representation, while it would have driven deeper the wedge that is destined to destroy the distinction between the county and the borough.

This was a very important question in Birmingham, where a rating franchise would have failed to enfranchise a single individual, owing to the operation of a local Act, which extended the principle of the Small Tenements Rating Act; and my articles upon the Bill, in which I called attention to its non-enfranchising character, and predicted that compound householder question which created so much difficulty in 1867, attracted considerable attention, not only in Birmingham, but in all the towns in which the journal circulated. Parliamentary reform was shelved, however, on account of the war with Russia, and I believe no one mourned the withdrawal of the Bill, both the Government and the House of Commons being glad of an excuse for not dealing with the subject, and the unenfranchised feeling nothing but contempt or resentment for such a measure as Lord John Russell had introduced.

The war, moreover, was popular, and the unenfranchised knew that their cause must gain from delay. A war demonstration was convened in St. Martin's Hall, and it was in assisting and reporting it that I first became acquainted with the operations of the Foreign Affairs Committees, instituted by David Urquhart.

"Some of Urquhart's party will be there," I was told, "and when those fellows get on their legs, you require to be one of the initiated to know what they are driving at. There will be a row."

I congratulated myself upon having a ticket for the platform when I saw how crowded the hall was, and how eager the throng seemed for fiery speeches. When the proceedings commenced, the popular feeling in favour of Turkey was strongly manifested; but when Mr. Collet, the editor of Urquhart's organ, raised the question of the restoration of Poland, it became evident that he was not so well understood by the meeting as Ernest Jones or Julian Harney would have been speaking upon that topic. Between the disadvantage which he laboured under of being, or seeming to be, opposed to the war, and the efforts of several gentlemen on the platform to prevent him from speaking, he had great difficulty in obtaining a hearing. Lord Harrington, who was in the chair, exerted himself to maintain order, and some of the gentlemen on the platform, including myself, strove to secure Mr. Collet an audience; but the uproar continued for some time, during which Mr. Collet remained standing, but desisted speaking through inability to make himself heard. Sir William (then Mr.) Tite, who was sitting next to me, was one of his most violent and persistent opponents.

"Sit down, Mr. Tite!" I at length exclaimed, grasping his arm as I spoke. "This is most unfair. You have no right to howl a man down because you don't agree with him."

The honourable member for Bath turned upon me sharply, with an angry expression of countenance; but he sat down, without giving vent to the resentment at my interference which he seemed to feel. Mr. Collet was then permitted to finish his speech, but the proceedings continued so stormy and confused, that nobody knew whether his amendment or the original resolution had been carried.

It was at this meeting that Sir Robert Peel, who then held the office of Secretary to the Admiralty, made the famous speech, in which he described himself as "an independent member of the Government." The designation was laughed at in the clubs, and much commented upon by the press; but there can be no doubt that it was honestly given, and correctly described the right honourable baronet's position. He was too honest and independent for office in those days, and, after exchanging the Admiralty for the Irish Office, he dropped out of the list of possible future Ministers. The statesmen of that day feared his honest, outspoken utterances, lest he should reveal something which they wished to conceal. I was present when a contention arose in the Select Committee on Public Contracts, as to something which had been done at the Admiralty while he was in office, and it was proposed that he should be called to clear up the matter. The Ministerial members were quivering with fear, lest, if the right honourable baronet was called, he might reveal more than the Government were willing to have known; and, after some whispering and laying together of heads, the more discreet Mr. Phinn was sent for instead.

Reporting Select Committees was an agreeable variation from the task which I often had to perform, of winnowing the grain from the chaff of official Blue Books and Parliamentary Papers. On one occasion, however, I got into collision with the late James Wilson, then Secretary to the Treasury, and was very near raising a question of breach of the privileges of Parliament. I was reporting the

Assay Committee, over which that gentleman presided, and which he or the Government, for some reason by no means obvious—unless the hypothesis may be ventured that he desired an exclusive report for his own paper—wished to be secret. No intimation to that effect had been given, however, and, as great importance was attached to the inquiry in Birmingham and Coventry, I should have paid no attention to it if there had been.

The inquiry was apparently an open one, the public being admitted below the bar, and reporters to the table which, in every committee-room, is assigned to them. On the second day, however, before the proceedings commenced, one of the witnesses, a watch manufacturer from a provincial town, informed Mr. Rose, clerk to the committee, that the evidence given by him on the first day had appeared in a local newspaper. Mr. Rose thereupon came round to the reporters' table, and asked me whether I was the reporter of the journal that had been mentioned.

"I am," I replied.

"Did you report the evidence taken on the first day of this inquiry?" he asked, regarding me austerely.

"I did," said I.

"Don't you know that to do so is a breach of privilege?" he inquired, with increasing severity.

"So is the publication of the debates," I rejoined, wondering what was to come next.

The equipoise of the official mind seemed to be upset for a moment by my cool audacity.

"The chairman desires that this inquiry shall be private," said Mr. Rose, when he had recovered from the shock, "and if you take any notes of to-day's evidence you will be turned out of the room."

At that moment Wilson entered, and the clerk left me, and, bending over the chair at the head of the horse-shoe-shaped table around which the committee sat, made a communication to him, the nature of which I had no difficulty in guessing.

"Clear the room!" said Wilson, sharply.

The witnesses in attendance and the score or so of listeners below the bar left the room, and I followed. In a few minutes the door was opened, and they flocked in again, but on my attempting to follow, I found the way barred by one of the messengers.

"I have orders not to admit you," said he.

"On what ground?" I inquired.

"It is the chairman's order," he replied.

"The chairman has no right to exclude me individually," said I. "The inquiry is an open one, and I demand admission."

The man seemed undecided as to the course he should adopt on finding me determined to enter, but on my grasping the handle of the door, he made a warning gesture with his hand.

"If you attempt to stop me, I shall charge you with an assault," said I.

"You must take your chance, then, if you will not be warned," he observed, withdrawing his hand.

Instead of returning to my seat at the reporter's table, I now stood below the bar, keeping my notebook in my pocket. In a few minutes I saw Mr. Rose whispering to the chairman, who immediately looked towards me.

"Are you the reporter who has been complained of?" he asked.

"Yes, sir," I replied.

"You have been desired to withdraw," he observed, in the tone of one who demands an explanation.

"This inquiry is an open one," I returned. "If you order the room to be cleared, I shall withdraw; but while the room is open to the public I claim the right to remain."

"You are not taking notes?"

"No, sir."

"Very well. The inquiry is, as you say, an open one; but you must not take any more notes."

There the matter dropped. I took no more notes, but I attended every meeting of the committee, and having a very retentive memory, I was enabled to report as correctly, though not quite so fully, as if I had sat at the reporters' table and taken notes. The witness who had complained had no evidence to give, and no one called attention to the fact that the evidence continued to be reported.

James Wilson ought to have been one of the last men to complain of publicity being given by the press to evidence taken by Parliamentary committees, even when there are Governmental reasons for desiring secrecy. His own hands were not clean. Journalistic competition renders it of great importance to obtain early or exclusive information upon any matter of public interest, and many are the devices resorted to for the purpose. The *modus operandi* is often an impenetrable mystery; but there was no mystery about the way in which the *Economist* was enabled to place before its readers, before the document had been issued, the Treasury warrant permitting the mixture of chicory with coffee, James Wilson being at the time proprietor of the *Economist* and Secretary to the Treasury.

Though the copies of the draught Report or Reports of Select Committees and Royal Commissions which are furnished to the members for reference during the discussion of its propositions bear an official notification that it is for their use only, the intimation is frequently disregarded; and, in some way or other, the substance of the Report almost invariably oozes out, and is communicated to the press before the Report is ready for issue. This does not necessarily imply a breach of confidence on the part of a member.

Though I had become familiar with many secret channels of information, and had been tolerably successful in availing of them, I was as much surprised as any experienced journalist can be at anything when I saw in the columns of the *Times* long extracts from the Report of the Public Schools Commission, at a time when I had been assured that it was not yet printed, and had failed to procure a sight of it, or any information as to its leading propositions. I had been watching for that Report for months. I knew that it was settled, and that proofs had long been in the hands of the Commismissioners; and I had learned only the day before that the delay was due to the absence from town of the Lord Chancellor, who had not yet returned the proof which had been forwarded to him. How a copy of the Report had got into the hands of the editor of the *Times* I could only surmise. The matter was brought before Parliament, however, and it then transpired that the Secretary to the Commission had, on receiving the Lord Chancellor's proof, sent a copy of the report to Printing House Yard by *mistake*, as the matter was represented by the Ministerial gentleman who explained it to the House.

On one well remembered occasion, when I had obtained permission to read an important document on the conditions of secrecy as to the source of my information, refraining from copying a single line, and returning it the same day, I was placed in a terrible predicament. On my way home I had called at the house of a brother journalist, to whom I had mentioned in professional confidence my possession of the paper, and at his solicitation I consented to leave it with him for a few hours. On applying for it, he startled me with the assertion that he had not got it, and that I must have inadvertently taken it away.

I knew not what to think. Could I have lost the paper? That hypothesis was dismissed in a moment. Then I must have carried it home. Thither I returned in hot haste; but the paper was nowhere to be found. My wife had not seen it. Perspiration stood in cold drops on my forehead as I thought of the possible consequences of the paper not being forthcoming when required. As it was not a printed document, but a roll of manuscript, of which, as far as I was aware, there was no duplicate in existence, there was no possibility of preventing discovery by the substitution of another copy.

Once more I hurried to my friend's house, where I asked the servant who admitted me whether I had a roll of paper in my hand when I left the house on the first occasion. I was reassured by the woman telling me that I had nothing in my hands when I went out; and, as I bounded up the stairs, I was met by my brother journalist, who greeted me, greatly to my relief, with the assurance that it was "all right." He had placed the roll of manuscript behind a sofa pillow on a gentleman being announced who had called on business, and afterwards had forgotten where he had put it, and thereupon endeavoured to persuade himself that it had not been in his possession. That he had some difficulty in doing so may be inferred from his making the search which resulted in the discovery of the paper where he had concealed it.

CHAPTER XVI.

THE HYDE PARK RIOTS.

Is it really a quarter of a century since the turf of Hyde Park was trampled by howling mobs, and the dwellers in Belgravia were admonished to go to church by the unwashed of Whitechapel? Time has flown rapidly, but there can be no mistake about the date. It was in the summer of 1855, when the war with Russia occupied public attention, almost to the exclusion of any other topic, that Lord Robert Grosvenor asked the House of Commons to discuss a bill which, according to the preamble, was to secure the better observance of the Lord's day. The end which the supporters of the measure desired to attain was good, but the means proposed were bad, and they could not well be otherwise.

If the majority of the nation were agreed as to the observance of Sunday, there would be no need of legislation upon the subject; and the absence of such agreement creates a difficulty in dealing with it which is greatly increased by the impracticability of devising a measure that shall be free from the odium which attaches to the making of "one law for the rich, and another for the poor." Lord Robert Grosvenor proposed to prohibit the running of railway trains and steamboats on Sundays, and to close every public place of refreshment from midnight on Saturday till Monday morning. The objectionable character of such a measure is not so obvious perhaps to dwellers in the country, or to those who know nothing of the conditions of life among the working classes of the large towns, as to the artisans and labourers and work-women who toil six days in unhealthy factories and crowded workshops, and live in a couple of rooms, or, as in tens of thousands of cases, in the one room which serves a whole family for sitting-room, bed-chamber, kitchen, and scullery. These, whether or not they attend a place of worship on Sunday, naturally ask why they should be debarred from a sight of the green fields on the only day they can look upon them, while the carriages of the rich convey them wherever they please to go; and why they should be compelled to take water with their Sunday dinner, while the rich indulged as freely as they pleased in wine and beer.

The results of the discussion of the Sunday bill were, therefore, such as might have been expected. The proposal to prohibit Sunday excursions and

Sunday beer produced a feeling of the deepest exasperation. By one of those widely diffused impulses which, in times of popular excitement, set multitudes in motion without previous concert, the masses of the metropolis poured into Hyde Park on the last Sunday in June, and, swarming upon and along the principal avenues, assailed the occupants of carriages with cries of "Go to church!" Many ladies were frightened, and some had their carriages driven homeward; but no disposition to riot was manifested until the following Sunday, when the mob in the park was estimated to number no fewer than 150,000 persons.

The consciousness of strength which the vastness of the gathering inspired, the extent to which the popular exasperation had been fanned during the preceding week, and the efforts at repression that were made by the police, then combined to produce a tumult which, in Paris or Madrid, might have resulted in the fall of the Ministry, perhaps of the Crown. The crowds were no longer content with advising the privileged orders to set the example of a purely religious observance of Sunday. They hissed and hooted such supporters of the obnoxious bill as they recognized, stopped every carriage, and allowed to proceed only those the occupants of which showed prayer-books as evidence that they were on their way to a place of worship.

Lord Palmerston was one of the many notabilities whose carriage was turned back. The newspapers stated that he was not recognized, but this is improbable, as he was one of the best known men in Parliament. The statement was probably a mere assumption, based on his supposed popularity, which, as far as the working classes were concerned, was very small.

The repeated but unsystematic efforts of the police to repress these disorderly proceedings had no other effect than to exasperate the mob, and aggravate an evil which they were powerless to prevent.

No attempt was made to clear the park, which probably would not have been done without the assistance of the military; whose services might, once called for, have been required elsewhere than in Hyde Park. All that the police did was to make wild rushes at intervals into the crowd, and use their staves upon heads, arms, and shoulders in the most violent and reckless manner. Many persons sustained serious injuries from these assaults, which caused the mob to give way for the moment at the point against which they were directed, and to which the multitude surged back when the police receded.

Scores of persons were arrested, and the station-houses were crowded to an extent which, combined with the savage mood of the constables who guarded them, made the sufferings of the prisoners scarcely less dreadful than those of the victims of Surajah Dowla in the "black hole" of Calcutta. The conduct of the police was afterwards made the subject of inquiry by a special commission, by whose Report it was severely censured.

On the afternoon of the second Sunday in July, wishing to form an independent judgment of the behaviour of the mob on the one hand, and of the police on the other, I proceeded to Hyde Park, seeing and hearing on my way enough to produce a strong impression upon my mind that, if the tactics of the guardians of order remained unchanged, the day would not close without a sanguinary conflict. Few of the men who were going the same way as myself were without sticks, and I heard many remarks as to the use that was to be made of them. In the park, several men and lads were carrying under their arms bundles of stout sticks, which they were selling to those who had gone unprovided with the means of defence; and there was an unmistakable air of resolve about the crowds that thronged the Long Drive and gathered on the greensward that foreboded mischief.

But the counsels of wisdom had prevailed, rather than the brutal suggestion of a cannonade offered in the House of Commons by a military member, and the conflict that had appeared to be impending was averted. No carriages appeared, and no attempt to disperse the mob was made by the police. The adage that it takes two to make a quarrel received a very forcible illustration. The multitude soon tired of thronging the railings, and scattered over the park.

Seeing a movement from all directions towards the magazine, I hurried to the spot, where I found a company of the guards under arms, and a momently increasing crowd gathering in front. Suddenly the officer in command cried "Fall in!" and in a moment every soldier was in his place, awaiting the next order. There was no movement, however, on either side; the attitude of both was that of anxious expectation, mingled on the part of many of the crowd with a feeling of curiosity.

Early in the evening, when the throng was fast diminishing, I left the park by Apsley Gate, and crossed the Green Park towards Westminster. The groups whom I passed seemed to be proceeding quietly homeward, but a numerous section was moving through Belgravia; and before I reached home I learned that the windows of a large number of the supporters of the Sunday bill had been broken, and some alarm created by the burning of a quantity of straw, which had been laid down before the house of the Archbishop of York.

On the following day Lord Robert Grosvenor withdrew the bill which had produced so much excitement, and prompted such an alarming irruption into the region of palatial mansions and aristocratic clubs; and thereupon the Sunday disturbances ceased, not without having increased the popular jealousy and mistrust of the higher orders, and created a precedent for the conversion of Hyde Park into the forum of the masses.

The precedent was not forgotten when Lord Palmerston introduced his unpopular Conspiracy Bill at the instigation of the French Emperor, who thereby forfeited the transitory gleam of favour which the English people had accorded him during the war with Russia. Before relating what I saw of the popular manifestations of that period, however, I must speak of an incident which occurred at the time of the Emperor's visit to London, and which has not been recorded by Mr. Blanchard Jerrold. On the night following the arrival of our imperial visitor in the metropolis, I was passing through one of the bye-streets in the vicinity of Leicester Square, when I passed a man whose bronzed face and grizzled moustaches I thought I recognized as the light of a lamp fell full upon his countenance on his stepping from a *café-restaurant* frequented by many of the French refugees.

"M. Alphonse?" said I, turning round the moment I had passed him.

That was not his name, but it will do as well as another.

"Ah!" he ejaculated, with a glance of half-recollection, "I think I have seen you at the gatherings of the Fraternal Democrats. There have been some ups and downs since those days, my friend."

"Did you see the Emperor?" I inquired, as I lighted a cigarette at his black pipe.

"*A bas l'assassin!*" he growled. "Let him take care. His crimes are not forgotten or forgiven by the men whom they have forced to expatriation. Let him take care when he goes to the City."

He nodded significantly as he uttered this implied threat, but I attached little importance to it.

"He bears a charmed life," I rejoined, laughing as I went on my way.

After the imperial visit to the Mansion House, there was a vague rumour that the Emperor was to have been shot on his way through the City, but that the intending assassin had been deterred from the attempt by the fear of injuring the Empress. The rumour might have been as difficult to trace to its source as was the absurd report of a later period, that the Prince Consort had been arrested and confined in the Tower, but I was made aware of it by its being mentioned to me by more than one person.

"You couldn't get the silver bullet," I remarked jocularly to the French refugee, on meeting him in Tichborne Street a few nights afterwards.

"I ? no," he rejoined, first elevating his eyebrows, and then shrugging his shoulders. "But I know an Italian who would have had a shot at him, but—"

"For fear of hurting the Empress," I said, interpolating the motive which had been assigned by rumour.

"Bah!" returned Alphonse, with a gesture of contempt for the idea. "But what chance was there with one of your cuirassiers of the guard riding on each side of the carriage? Those big fellows were as good as a shield to the man."

The attempt of Pianori closely followed the Emperor's return to Paris, and there was probably not an hour of his life during the ten years between the siege of Rome and the declaration of war against Austria in which he was safe from the assassin's aim.

He had committed more perjuries than one, and the oath of the Carbonari was one not to be violated with impunity.

That there were Italian refugees in London capable of meditating the design which Alphonse had attributed to one of them, and of attempting its execution if a favourable opportunity had been offered, was proved by an event that occured a few months after the attempt of Pianori. Five Italians were, at mid-day, in a coffee-house in Rupert Street. Their names were Foschini, Rudio, Rossi, Chiesa, and

Rouelli, the last being the waiter of the place, which was frequented chiefly by his compatriots. Suddenly Rossi cried out that he was stabbed, and a blood-stained dagger was seen in the hand of Foschini.

Then a struggle ensued, in which Rudio, Chiesa, and Rouelli were severely wounded; and Foschini quitted the house, walked quietly down the street, and was never seen or heard of afterwards, so far as ever became known to the public.

The affair created a considerable sensation, but it remains to this day a profound mystery to all but those whom it personally concerned. The efforts of the police to trace Foschini were unavailing; the wounded men evinced a reluctance to speak of the affray which indicated the existence of something that they wished to conceal; and, as they all eventually recovered, no judicial investigation was made.

All the circumstances point, however, to a secret society, of which the men concerned in the fray were members; and those who have read Wilkie Collins' sensational story of "The Woman in White" will have no difficulty, if at all acquainted with the history of secret societies, and especially of the Carbonari, in finding the clue to the mystery.

It was about this time that I was startled one evening by hearing a hoarse voice loudly proclaiming that the Emperor of the French had been shot dead in his carriage while on his way to the opera.

I put on my hat, and hurried to the residence of the London correspondent of a Liverpool journal, to whom I communicated the startling intelligence.

"It may be true," said he, with an air of thought. "There is nothing, indeed, more likely. True or not, it will probably be his fate, sooner or later."

Next morning the absence of any telegram from Paris confirming the announcement proved its falsity.

The "hoarse unfeathered nightingale" by whom it was made was an old man, who, as I afterwards learned, was in the habit of hawking "catchpenny" accounts of similar character about the streets after the hour at which the last ordinary edition of the evening papers appeared.

The air was full of false reports at that period, and for some time afterwards. I was walking quickly along Lambeth Walk one morning, on my way to Westminster, when my ears caught the words "arrested last night, and sent to the Tower," as I passed a group of workmen who were standing at the corner of a street. As I was wondering as I went on my way who could have been the object of this attention on the part of the Home Secretary, I heard the name of the Prince Consort mentioned by a shopkeeper, who was in earnest conversation with his neighbour before his window. What could it mean? I glanced eagerly at the contents-bills of the morning papers, but saw not a line that enlightened me.

"It can't be true," I heard a mechanic say, as I reached the foot of Westminster Bridge. "I read the paper while I was having my breakfast, and there isn't a word about it."

The speaker was one of a group of workmen who were reading a bill setting forth the contents of a morning journal, and I paused, in hope of hearing something more.

"Perhaps they have kept it out of the papers," observed one of the men.

"What do they say he has done?" inquired another. "That's what I want to get at."

"Intriguing with Russia!" replied the second speaker. "Making himself a tool of Menzikoff! That's what them blessed Germans are always a-doing."

Later in the day I encountered the London reporter of a provincial Conservative journal.

"Have you heard this extraordinary story about the Prince?" I inquired.

"Heard it as soon as I was up," he replied. "That he was arrested last night, and sent to the Tower. That was all, at first; but before I could get a paper, the story was improved by the explanation that Lord Palmerston had discovered an intrigue in which the Prince was engaged with Russia against the interests of England."

From another person to whom I mentioned the

rumour I received a similar explanation, with the difference that Lord Palmerston, being supposed to be a tool of the Russian Foreign Office, was said to have concocted the charge against the Prince, whom he found an obstacle to the coercion of the Queen into the policy of the Cabinet of St. Petersburg.

How the rumour originated was a mystery. So far as I was able to trace it, the *canard* was hatched in the Lower Marsh, but whether it emanated from some Foreign Affairs Committee, or was concocted by some mischievous idler for his own amusement, will probably never be known. It was no Stock Exchange hoax, no exaggeration of club gossip. It had spread all over Lambeth, and reached Westminster, long before the Exchange was open, or legislators had left their beds.

The rumour of a few years later, that Lord Palmerston had died that morning, was first heard in the City, between three and four in the afternoon. The veteran statesman was suffering at the time from a severe attack of gout, which, at his advanced age, gave an air of credibility to the story. But, on making inquiry at Cambridge House, I found that, so far from being dead, he was so much improved in health that he had gone out for a drive.

"There will be a tremendous crash when he does go," observed the London correspondent of the *Albion*, when I communicated to him the result of my inquiries at Cambridge House. "The system which he represents will end with him, and who the coming man is to be there is not a sign to indicate."

"There is Gladstone," said I, naming the statesman in whom I had more confidence than in any other.

"The country will not have him," he rejoined. "Some Whig stop-gap will be found for a time; but the man who can hold the reins as long as Palmerston has held them has got to be found. He is not discernible on either side of the House."

Palmerston's political vitality was as remarkable as the physical vigour which he preserved to his latest years. Dismissed from office by the Queen for an act which should have precluded him from ever setting foot in Downing Street again, he held his head as high as before, and was able, in 1858, to bring in a measure at variance equally with the traditional policy of the country and the sympathies of that generation. The Conspiracy Bill was a bold experiment in what it is now the fashion to call Imperialism—an insolent expression of careless disregard of the popular feeling, and of cynical contempt for his supporters in Parliament. It was a piece of exceptional legislation in favour of a perjured and blood-stained usurper, who had ten years previously enrolled himself on the side of an unrighteous combination to exclude from political power the people among whom he had found a refuge; and it was submitted to Parliament by a Minister who had aimed at a dictatorship in having, to use the emphatic words of Lord John Russell, " passed by the Crown, and put himself in the place of the Crown." Could Polignac or Metternich have been bolder, or more blind?

The attempt to make Parliament a machine for registering the decrees of the French Emperor roused a spirit all over the country which Palmerston must have supposed to be extinct. The masses of the metropolis swarmed into Hyde Park again, and demonstrations against the bill were made, Sunday after Sunday, at which stronger language was used than I had heard since 1848. That England should be stigmatized as "a den of conspirators" by the mouthpiece of a man who had shared her hospitality, and made "a den of conspirators" of every place in which he had lived, before and after; that the Government, instead of resenting such language, should assume a position so opposite to that which the admirers of Lord Palmerston claimed for him, of being "a truly British Minister," and act as the instruments of Napoleon, was a situation which roused the resentment of every one in whose heart there glowed one spark of patriotism.

The Conspiracy Bill so closely concerned the foreign refugees in London, especially those of

French nationality, that I was not surprised, when I went to Hyde Park to inform myself as to the aspect of affairs, to observe the neighbourhoods of Soho and Leicester Square well represented in the crowds assembled there. It was said that the spies of M. Pietri were there also to watch them, and the hunting of foreigners, who were denounced as such, furnished the " roughs," who hang on the skirts of every popular demonstration, with the most exciting episodes of the agitation.

I was walking on one of those Sunday afternoons on the north side of the Park, when a man with a pale scared face and a torn coat dashed past me like a hunted deer. As I turned to look after him, I heard a shout, and in another moment a score or two of men and boys rushed on in the track of the terror-stricken fugitive, yelling in tones that expressed mingled indignation and disgust. I saw the man run down, and hastened to the spot, where I found him in the centre of an excited crowd, which had already received a considerable augmentation of numbers. The white-faced fugitive, whose garments were in shreds, was gasping and gesticulating; but no angry hands were now raised against him, for a constable stood by his side, whether for his protection only I am unable to say, as contradictory stories circulated on the edge of the throng with regard to the matter which had provoked the rough treatment which he had received from his pursuers.

In the midst of the excitement created by his unpopular proposition, Lord Palmerston resigned. He had for once miscalculated his strength. He had been so long the idol of the shopkeepers, and so successful in overcoming opposition to his will, whether from the Crown, as in 1851, or from Parliament, as in 1857, that he could see no reason why he should not continue to rule to the end of the chapter. But there was a weak point in his position which overweening confidence in its strength had caused him to overlook. The consideration that no very great amount of statesmanship is required in a Minister to whom the constituencies are willing to give *carte blanche,* on the sole condition of attempting no radical changes that might disturb trade, and especially of not " opening the flood-gates of democracy," does not seem to have entered his calculations. The policy was easy, and its exponent might as well be a Conservative as a sham Liberal—a Granville or a Clarendon as a Palmerston.

This indifference to party extended to the working classes, but had grown up in their minds from a different cause. These saw that they had no more to expect from one than from the other of the two great parties, and regarded with indifference the rise and fall of Ministers that, whether called Liberal or Conservative, were equally opposed to their enfranchisement. There was not a statesman, not a leading man in Parliament, to whom they could give their entire confidence. Mr. Bright's utterances on the franchise question were too undecided. He never seemed to know—certainly no one else ever knew—whether he advocated manhood suffrage or household suffrage, or a suffrage limited to householders who paid a certain amount of rent.

This unhealthy state of the public mind was a source of anxiety to every thoughtful man. Parties no longer held different principles, and it seemed that they could be saved from confusion only by their disintegration, and the formation of new combinations from their elements. The middle classes were absorbed in the pursuit of gain; the working classes were without political power. Even the attempts, as feeble as they were fitful, which the House of Commons made from time to time, to deal in some fashion with the franchise question, served only to threaten with obliteration the landmarks of the Constitution.

To those who know no more of the working classes than could be gathered from a very superficial view, there seemed at this time to be an amount of apathy on the part of the unenfranchised to the questions raised by Mr. Bright and Mr. Locke King, which was strangely at variance with the idea that they earnestly desired the franchise. But this was a mistake, and one which could be made only by those who misunderstood the bearings of the question upon different sections of the people. There was certainly no popular excitement, for the realities of life press too heavily upon the working man for him to become enthusiastic about trifles, and indulge in jubilation about matters which have no direct and immediate interest for him. There was not much in any of the measures of Parliamentary reform successively produced by Lord John Russell, Mr. Bright, and Mr. Locke King, to prompt the workmen of London and the large towns, which lead the van in such movements, to shout and throw up their caps. Every measure that made rating a necessary preliminary to registration could be regarded by working men as only an exemplification of "how not to do it."

CHAPTER XVII.

THE LAST YEARS OF PALMERSTON'S DICTATORSHIP.

THE climax of Parliamentary subserviency to the Minister, which the constituencies acquiesced in by condoning, seemed to be reached when a deputation of the House of Commons, composed of men calling themselves Liberals, waited upon Lord Palmerston with a humble request that he would diminish the pressure of taxation. The dictator reminded them, with almost contemptuous curtness, and in words which might have been more strongly emphasized, and yet been made pardonable by their truthfulness, that *they* were the guardians of the public purse, and that they had sanctioned the expenditure which caused the pressure of taxation of which they complained. If those men had been real representatives of the people, and had done their duty, they would have reduced the estimates, and thus rendered a diminution of taxation possible, instead of voting the expenditure without opposition, and then begging the Minister to relieve the nation from the pressure of taxation.

Nothing could have shown more plainly than this incident the need of Parliamentary reform; and the symptoms of a revival of popular agitation were significant enough to induce Lord Palmerston to set in motion the machinery by which the scare of a French invasion was got up, as a means of diverting public attention from a crisis which both parties in that corrupt Parliament wished to defer as long as might be possible. It is a curious chapter of the national history, and one not very pleasant to contemplate, upon which I am looking back while writing these observations. Whether there were wire-pullers on the French side of the Channel as well as on this may never be known, but the relations between Palmerston and Buonaparte render it very probable that the gasconading of certain French colonels was the result of collusion. There can be no doubt, however, that the chief promoter of the scare did not believe that there was any reason for it, and that many of the magnates of the land either shared his non-belief or disliked the idea of French conquest less than that of democratic rule.

When the scare produced the volunteer movement, Lord Palmerston, who proposed to expend ten millions upon coast defences, endeavoured to throw a wet blanket upon the national enthusiasm, though there were in England only a tenth of the troops which Sir John Burgoyne had pronounced to be necessary for any resistance to invasion that could be made with the slightest prospect of success. Prominent members of the aristocracy evinced the utmost hostility to the movement. When Henry Drummond and others, who argued that, if the danger really existed, the people should be armed to meet it, proposed to enrol all who offered; to uniform them in belted gaberdines or Garibaldian shirts, and arm them with pikes until a sufficient number of rifles could be provided; the proposition produced a thrill of fear throughout the upper ten thousand. The late Lord Lyttelton protested against the admission of working men into volunteer corps, which would have constituted a useless expense without them; and the Duke of Rutland declared that, if working men were armed, he would plant cannon before Belvoir Castle, and raise a corps for its protection among his dependents. Patriotism prevailed over aristocratic fears, however, and the volunteer force remained when the scare was forgotten.

Close upon the volunteer movement came the excitement produced by the rejection by the House of Lords of the bill for the repeal of the paper duties. Since the time when the first Reform Bill was rejected by that assembly—a time which the progress since achieved seems to have pushed back into the dark ages—no question had produced such a profound agitation in political circles. The impression that the Lords had infringed upon the privileges of the Commons was very general, and the situation was felt to be a grave one. Very strong language was used in some of the Liberal journals. I remember using some myself; for, though the Commons represented only a minority of the people, the minority and the majority were of one mind for once, and it was obvious that a collision between the two Houses, if pushed to extremity, must tend to the advantage of the unenfranchised.

But the strongest language used by the press was equalled, if not exceeded, by that held by some at least of the speakers at a gathering of Liberal members of the House of Commons, privately convened at the King's Arms Tavern, in New Palace Yard. The room was crowded, and, with three exceptions, only members of the Lower House were present. The exceptions were Lord Teynham, Mr. Lucraft, and myself. The meeting had been so hastily and quietly convened that I had heard of it only an hour before the members assembled, and there was a stir of surprise when a young man with an earnest and intelligent countenance stepped upon the hearthrug, and announced the unknown name of Lucraft, since well-known as that of an active and popular member of the London School Board.

Mr. Lucraft was listened to with an attention which one of his order would not have received from such a gathering, at that time, under other and less exceptional circumstances. His speech, both as to matter and manner, was certainly one of the best, if not the very best, that was delivered on that occasion. He was earnest, without being hurried by his enthusiasm into intemperate language such as was used by an Irish M.P., now a peer, who, immediately recollecting that I was taking notes, turned his head over his left shoulder, and said to me, in a subdued tone, "Don't put that down."

The storm passed by, and Parliament again took up the church-rate question, which had been urged upon its attention any time within memory. I had few opportunities of attending the debates at that period, and I heard the greatest orators of the House of Commons for the first time on one of the Wednesday afternoons devoted to the consideration of bills introduced by independent members. Mr. Disraeli displayed more brilliance than depth or solidity; he seemed to be aiming at a rhetorical display, rather than earnestly striving for a principle, or assiduously labouring to convince his opponents. Mr. Gladstone disappointed me; his manner was cold and constrained, and his calmly flowing periods were neither embellished with the rhetorical graces of the Conservative leader, nor made eloquent by the earnestness which was impressed upon every sentence of the powerful oration of Mr. Bright. But the honourable member for Birmingham electrified me. He impressed me with the idea that he was the only speaker who felt sufficient interest in the issue of the debate to speak earnestly; and the man who is in earnest is always eloquent, however uncultured his mind and rude his language.

"He is the greatest orator in the House," I remarked to a Liberal journalist, on leaving the gallery. "If there was really a Liberal party in the House, he ought to be its leader; and he might be, if the few real Liberals would separate themselves from the sham ones, and form a popular party, before which the shams would have to retire, or coalesce with the Conservatives."

"What would be gained?" rejoined the gentleman to whom I made this remark. "The House cannot be better than the nation it is taken from, and the more you widen the basis of representation the more depressing will be the dead level of mediocrity which the House will present."

"That result would not follow as a matter of course," said I. "But if it did, an assembly of mediocrities representing the whole of the people would be infinitely better for the well-being of the nation than an assembly of master-minds representing only a small minority. Desirable as it is that the representatives of the people should be of intellect and culture, it is still more desirable that the people should not be *misrepresented* by clever men who do not understand the social questions which are pressing for solution, and whose views and feelings can never harmonize with those of the masses. Mr. Disraeli is one of the cleverest men in the House; but, if you concede, as you must, that he knows less of the wants and wishes of the people of Lambeth than Mr. Williams, you must admit that Mr. Williams is a better *representative* of Lambeth than Mr. Disraeli would be."

I have reproduced this conversation because the view expressed by myself is one which is apt to escape the cognizance of cultured minds, and which will require earnest consideration in the future. Manhood suffrage will undoubtedly give us an assembly of mediocrities, if men of intellect and culture do not make themselves acquainted with the social economics of the working classes, and thus qualify themselves to deal with the questions which must soon come to the front.

At the time of which I am writing, however, the franchise question seemed to be shelved by general consent until the death of Lord Palmerston should break the spell with which he seemed to have bound the House of Commons, and which should and may have caused the unenfranchised to pray daily that he might be speedily released from the cares and troubles of this life.

Journalists, with rare exceptions, endeavour to follow, rather than to direct, the current of public opinion, except when the latter course is recommended to their consideration by golden arguments. During the dull years immediately preceding the death of Lord Palmerston, when the invasion scare had subsided, and the political vitality of the nation remained dormant, it often became necessary to explore the untrodden fields of blue-book literature in quest of suggestions for articles, foreign affairs being always safe subjects, and commercial questions always welcome to a commercial people. To wade through hundreds of pages of most uninviting matter, perhaps heavily charged with statistics, is not a congenial task; but it is sometimes possible to gather the raw material of a very readable article from one of those azure-covered volumes, or even from the small fry of Parliamentary issues known as "white papers."

I had at this time transferred my services from a Birmingham to a Liverpool journal, the Liberalism of which was of a much less advanced type; and hence arose a more frequent employment of my pen upon commercial questions and foreign affairs. One day, when I was at the office of the Consul-general of the republic of Uruguay, his excellency entered the room in which I was sitting, with a note in his hand, which, being very busy, he asked me to answer, as the messenger was waiting.

The note informed me that a gentleman in the hydrographical department of the Admiralty being puzzled as to the geographical position of Colonia, had sent a messenger across to the offices of the Geographical Society, in Whitehall Place, for the information required, which it might have been thought would have been procurable there, if anywhere. There was no one there, however, who could say where Colonia was to be found on the map, and hence the application to the Monte Videan consulate. I wrote a brief note, informing the hydrographical gentleman that Colonia was a port of Uruguay. This did not suffice, however, for the messenger presently returned with a second note, asking for the further information, whether Uruguay was an independent State, or a province of the Argentine Confederation!

The official ignorance of American geography which was thus brought under my notice, and which suggests that the examination of candidates for Government clerkships might have been introduced at a much earlier period with advantage to the public service, was the cause at one time of a serious dispute between the British Government and the republic of Honduras. As the questions involved are not generally known, and I acted at the time as the secretary of the accredited agent of Honduras in London, a brief statement of them may not be uninteresting to some of my readers, and will not be altogether irrelevant to the narrative.

The reader knows, of course, that there is a British possession called Belize, but more commonly British Honduras; and a glance at any map of Central America will discover, in the Gulf of Honduras, a small island called Roatan, distant about a hundred and fifty miles from Belize, and less than fifty from the coast of Honduras. This little island was uninhabited until, some years before the dispute in question arose, a score or so of coloured people from Jamaica settled upon it; and when, shortly afterwards, a British frigate happened to touch at it to obtain supplies, the captain, finding it occupied by British subjects, and being ignorant of its history, took possession of it in the name of the Queen, and hoisted the British flag upon it. On his report to the Admiralty of what he had done, the matter was communicated to the Colonial Office, and thereupon the island was formally declared a British colony, and a dependency of British Honduras.

The Government at Comayagua, on being informed of what had taken place, at once claimed the island, on the ground that it had been, under the Spanish dominion, a dependency of the province of Honduras, which was included in the viceroyalty of Guatemala; and, consequently, that it must follow the fortunes of Honduras, and not those of Belize, which had originally been a province of the viceroyalty of Mexico.

Many communications on the subject passed between the Earl of Clarendon, who then held the seals of the Foreign Office, and the representative of the republic of Honduras in this country. It was, at the outset, contended by the former that the island of Roatan pertained to Belize, and had belonged to Great Britain from the time when that territory was ceded by Spain. It was shown, however, from old maps and official documents, that this was a mistake, and that the term British Honduras, which had contributed, if it did not directly lead, to the error, was an official misnomer. The evidence was too clear to be resisted, and Lord Clarendon negotiated a treaty between the United Kingdom and the republic of Honduras, by which the island of Roatan was surrendered to its rightful owners.

It is not easy, however, to obtain a hearing for the correction of geographical errors, and Belize continues to be called British Honduras. But then our statesmen have not been required to pass an examination in geography by the Dean's Yard examiners, and, as Cobden long ago complained, they have learned more at the universities and public schools about Troy and the Ilissus than about Central America.

It was while my pen had to range over events in progress all over the world, from the interminable Schleswig-Holstein question to the war in Paraguay, through the dearth of home subjects which interested Liverpudlian readers, that I became concerned in one of the most extraordinary transactions with which my journalistic experiences ever made me acquainted. I was asked by the London correspondent of the journal upon which I was engaged to write an article advocating the doubling of the duty on chicory, in order to check its excessive use in the mixture with coffee which had been authorized by the Treasury warrant referred to in a former chapter.

Having reported the Parliamentary inquiry into the adulterations of food, beverages, and drugs, which had been presided over by Mr. Scholefield, I was conversant with this subject, and able, therefore, to write intelligently about it. On the appearance of the article, slip copies of it were sent to the London daily papers, most of which inserted it. Then I was asked to write another, which was similarly made to go the round of the press, urging the advantage of the proposed augmentation of duty to the trade and revenue of the country, as the importation of coffee would increase in the same ratio as that of chicory would diminish.

When the question had been ventilated in the newspapers for some time, a deputation of wholesale dealers in coffee waited upon Mr. Gladstone, who was then Chancellor of the Exchequer, and represented to him the advantages that would accrue to the revenue, the trade, and the consumers from the proposed augmentation of duty to the extent of 100 per cent. An agitation for an increase of taxation is, I believe, unique; and Mr. Gladstone might have been excused if he had suspected that a keen regard for other interests than those of the revenue and the public was at the bottom of the movement. He was ignorant, it is to be presumed, of the real facts of the case, which were known to only a few persons, and were not allowed to transpire. He acceded, therefore, to the request of the deputation, and the duty on chicory was doubled.

The largest importer of chicory in this country had a very large stock of that commodity at the time when the policy of doubling the duty was first mooted, and he had conceived the idea of making a fortune at one stroke by obtaining possession of all that was procurable, and then forcing up the price. The first step to that end was the creation of a certain amount of public opinion in favour of the augmentation of the duty through the agency of the press; the second was the bringing a gentle pressure to bear upon the Chancellor of the Exchequer through the medium of some of the principal importers of coffee, whose commercial interests made them, consciously or unconsciously, the ready instruments of the speculator.

The Budget resolutions having been adopted by the House of Commons, the merchant who had been chief wire-puller in the business paid the old rate of duty on his immense stock of chicory, which he afterwards sold at the enhanced price to which the commodity was raised by the doubling of the duty, the profits of the transaction amounting, according to a statement that was made to me by a gentleman likely to be well informed, to no less than 70,000*l*.

CHAPTER XVIII.

THE DAWN OF A NEW ERA.

The death of Lord Palmerston dissolved the spell which had hung over the Liberal party for so many years, and had held even large sections of the nation in its thrall. Its announcement was like a thunderclap, startling old Whigs and Tories from the rest for which Lord Russell had exhorted them to be thankful, and clearing the political atmosphere of the miasma engendered by so long a period of unhealthy stagnation. The nation roused itself as from a Rip Van Winkle slumber of years, shook off the dews that stiffened its limbs, and entered upon a new term of existence.

The ministerial changes consequent upon the veteran statesman's demise occupied every journalistic pen on the day after its announcement. Though the event had been expected for several years, it found few persons prepared to indicate his successor with any degree of confidence.

"Who can tell?" said the London correspondent

of a Liverpool paper, when I sought to elicit his views on the subject. "His death will break up the Liberal party, and let loose the forces he has so long restrained; but as to a Government that would last three months, I don't know how it can be formed."

"I expect Lord John Russell will be the man," I observed.

"If the Queen is allowed to consult her own inclinations, her choice will be Lord Granville," said he.

"Lord Granville is an admirable President of the Council," I rejoined, "but he has not the stuff in him that is required in a Prime Minister. Gladstone is the coming man, I think; but his time has not come yet. In the present situation, the most likely man seems to be Lord Russell."

"It is precisely because he seems the most likely that it will not be him," returned my colleague. "Nothing happens but the unforeseen."

Some of my journalistic brethren must have felt, after they had written their leaders and London letters, as doubtful of the event as the sporting prophets who have indicated the probable winner of the Derby or the St. Leger, and find that they have named horses not selected by any other of the fraternity. My own selections were Lord Russell for the Premiership, Lord Clarendon for the Foreign

Office, and Mr. Gladstone for the Chancellorship of the Exchequer; and the announcement accurately foreshadowed the event.

To myself, and to many thousands, the assumption by Mr. Gladstone of the leadership of the Liberal party in the House of Commons seemed to promise the inauguration of a new era. It was known that he was as favourable to the revision and enlargement of the representation of the people in Parliament as Palmerston had been opposed to such changes, and the working classes hailed his accession to the Premiership with gladness and hope. Those ameliorations of the laws for which they had looked in vain during so many years of Whig rule, when electoral reform was said to be deferred in favour of legal reforms that were only talked about, had to be preceded by the enfranchisement of the class whose welfare required them; and Mr. Gladstone, on his part, was conscious that he could not carry the important measures which he contemplated without first strengthening his hands by a considerable extension of the franchise and redistribution of seats.

The situation differed very materially, however, from that which existed in 1831-2. Then the Commons and the people were agreed, and the only obstacle to the realization of the Ministerial scheme of Parliamentary reform was the antagonism of the

Lords, which, if pushed to extremity, could be overcome by the creation of Peers who would support the propositions of the Government. In 1866 the Commons were as much opposed to electoral changes as the Lords; and, if they persisted in their antagonism to changes which the people desired, the Constitution would be tied up in a Gordian knot which might have to be severed by the sword.

This was a possible contingency, however, which it was too early to touch upon in type, while the measure of Parliamentary reform to be proposed by the Russell-Gladstone Ministry was unknown, and the pliability of the House of Commons untested. My hope of the immediate success of a reforming policy was very faint, however, for it was easy to foresee that any measure that was small enough to find favour with the worst House that was ever elected would prove too small to satisfy the unenfranchised majority of the people. What the Radicals most feared was, that the measure would be made small enough to induce the House to accept it, in view of the alternative of having to accept a much more comprehensive one in the following session; and that then, in the absence of any efficient organization of the unenfranchised, the question would be considered settled for another quarter of a century.

It appeared to me more probable, however, that

Mr. Gladstone would not consent to the production of a measure so small as to be self-stultifying, and that the coming Reform Bill would be only just small enough to enable its promoters to claim for it the character of a moderate measure, and yet large enough to cause the House of Commons to reject it. Regarding the fall of the Ministry as a less serious calamity than the indefinite postponement of the complete enfranchisement of the people, I thought much more of the probable consequences of the rejection of the measure than of the possible results of its becoming law. Would the responsible advisers of the Sovereign counsel her to dissolve Parliament? Was there any prospect of a Radical majority being elected by the existing constituencies? If the House, representing the minority of the nation, would not yield, would the majority submit to their exclusion? These were some of the questions which I asked myself.

The measure produced was a very moderate one. Mr. Gladstone probably thought that it was mild enough to be accepted by the most reactionary House that had ever been elected by that generation, and that it would suffice to give him a majority that would enable him to deal successfully with the Irish question. But the Ministerial majority that Palmerston had commanded would not give its adhesion to Mr. Gladstone, unless he would consent to walk in his predecessor's footsteps. Mr. Horsman, Mr. Bouverie, Mr. Lowe, and thirty or forty more, seceded from the Liberal ranks, and proclaimed their resolve to oppose to the utmost any proposition for the enfranchisement of the working classes.

Mr. Bright compared the seceders to the followers of David when he retired to the cave of Adullam; "and every one that was in distress, and every one that was in debt, and every one that was discontented, gathered themselves unto him."[1] As the new Tory-Whig party had no leader, witty Mr. Bernal Osborne likened it to a Skye terrier. "You can't tell," said he, "which is the head, and which is the tail." The reactionists would perhaps have been without a name even, as well as without a leader, if Mr. Bright's description of them had not suggested the term Adullamites, which I believe I was the first to apply to them, in an article which I wrote for the Liverpudlian organ of moderate and independent Liberalism on the day after the debate.

The bill being defeated by the combination of the Conservatives and the Adullamites, the Russell-Gladstone Ministry resigned, and left their opponents to stand or fall before the current of popular feeling which was beginning to set in.

The diluted character of the Liberalism of the

[1] 1 Samuel xxii. 2.

middle classes of Liverpool rendered it a matter of some difficulty for me to treat the question of Parliamentary reform in a satisfactory manner. Both the Conservatism and the Liberalism of the Liverpudlians are of a very moderate type, and Lord Stanley would probably have been a more acceptable Minister to them at that time than either Lord Salisbury or Mr. Gladstone.

"Gladstone is not popular in Liverpool," I was told. "Dwell upon the muddle into which the conflict of parties is bringing the question, and the anomalies which the bill would leave untouched. All that will be safe; but deal very cautiously with the 'flesh and blood' argument. Indeed, the safest way will be to give no opinion of your own at all; but contrast the conflicting opinions expressed in Parliament, so as to show the impracticability of settling the question."

At this time, however, I was also writing the leaders for a Shrewsbury journal, representing the moderate Liberalism of the district, which was of a rather Whiggish type, qualified by the extent of its circulation in the border districts of Wales, where the Methodistic tendencies of the population influenced in some degree its treatment of Church questions. In discussing the situation, both before and after the resignation of the Russell-Gladstone Ministry, for my Salopian and Welsh readers, the disorganization which had been created in the ranks of the Liberal party by the Adullamite secession was favourable to the direction in which I aimed at guiding them. Before they could recover from the stunning effects of such successive blows as the death of Palmerston, the promulgation of a Reform Bill, the disruption of their party, and the defeat of its leaders, I had, I believe, convinced them that Parliamentary reform was a necessity of the times, and that the Adullamites were the worst enemies of the Constitution and the Crown.

After the Russell-Gladstone Ministry had resigned, I ventured to draw attention, in the Liverpool paper, to the possible danger of a House of Commons representing only a small minority of the nation refusing to enact measures demanded by the majority. I argued that, if the opposition to such measures came from the Crown, it could be overcome by the power of the Commons to refuse supplies; and if it proceeded from the Lords, as in 1831, by the creation of new peers, pledged to support the Ministerial propositions; but, if it came from the Commons, there was no remedy short of revolution, the theory of the Constitution being that that House represented the entire nation.

This argument was a novel one, to that generation at least, and it attracted considerable attention, both in and beyond the district in which the journal circulated that gave it publicity. Thoughtful men, whether Liberals or Conservatives, who had studied the working of the Constitution, acknowledged its cogency; Radicals, whether thinkers or not, were pleased with it as one that would be likely to impress the minds of the ruling classes with a due sense of the danger of an obstinate resistance to the popular will.

David Urquhart did me the honour of republishing the article in the *Diplomatic Review*, and making it the ground of a characteristically intemperate attack upon me in that publication, in which I was stigmatized as "either an imbecile or a traitor." The House of Commons, according to Urquhart, was powerless; so was the House of Lords; so was the Crown. The only real power in the State was that of the Minister, who was a tool of the Cabinet of St. Petersburg.

Knowing that the publication in which this outrageous attack appeared had a very limited circulation, being read by very few persons outside the Foreign Affairs Committees, I took no notice of it; but some years afterwards, when I called at the office to make an inquiry concerning the manner in which Urquhart proposed to deal with my letter on the extraordinary statements of the Abbé Defourny, mentioned in a former chapter, I recalled the matter to the mind of the gentleman whom I met there, and informed him that I was the writer of the article upon which Urquhart had poured out the vials of his wrath.

"You were given a choice of epithets," he observed, with a smile.

"That is of no consequence," I rejoined. "The serious aspect of the charge consists in the light which it throws upon the manner in which the like accusation has been hurled by Mr. Urquhart against more distinguished men. By an 'imbecile or a traitor' it was intended to be conveyed that I was either too shallow-minded to be conscious that I was playing into the hands of Russia, or that I had taken a bribe from that Power. Now, if Mr. Urquhart can be so egregiously mistaken in my case, may he not be equally wrong with regard to Palmerston, Kossuth, Cavour, and Mazzini?"

"Every one," was the reply, "who acts so as to serve the purposes of Russia, whether consciously or unconsciously, is a Russian agent."

"That is intelligible," said I. "It is a pity that the explanation is not appended, as a note, to every denunciation fulminated from East Temple Chambers. It would serve to show the value of the denunciation, which may be the reason why the explanation is not given. But, by the same process of reasoning, Mr. Urquhart might, in a certain concatenation of circumstances, be stigmatised as a

Russian agent, as 'an imbecile or a traitor,' with as much justice as he has accused others of being tools of the Cabinet of St. Petersburg."

"I can't imagine such a case," he observed.

"Suppose," said I—" it requires a little straining of probabilities, I admit—suppose the patriotic labours of the Foreign Affairs Committees resulting in the restoration to the Privy Council of the functions exercised by that body in the days of the Tudors, and the intestine troubles that might be expected to result from the change prompting Russia to avail of that opportunity to invade England."

"That is a view of the matter which I cannot admit," he rejoined. "We advocate a return to the ancient form of the Constitution, which would prevent or punish treason; while you support a system which gives impunity to treason by substituting a Minister, responsible only to men the majority of whom are his avowed and pledged partisans, for Councillors responsible to the Crown."

"But not to the people," said I.

"Oh, you are mistaken!" he returned quickly, and with an air of superiority of knowledge. "The will of the people was successfully asserted again and again."

"The will of the barons was," I rejoined. "When the masses strove to assert their rights, king and barons combined to put them down. What guarantee was there that legislation would be in accordance with either the will or the welfare of the nation? Whether the Cabinet be an innovation or not, is it to be taken for granted that the system of government by the Crown, with the advice of the Privy Council, would be as applicable to the England of the nineteenth century as to the England of the sixteenth? What legislation in the interests of the people would be possible under that system?"

"What would be the difficulty?" he asked.

"Parliament," I continued, "has now to deal with questions which the Tudors and the Stuarts would not allow to be discussed; and the House of Commons would not submit to be snubbed now as it was by Elizabeth. The Cabinet represents the House, as the House, in theory at least, represents the people; but the Privy Council might represent only the minority of the House. Even if all parties were represented in it, every important measure would be the result of a compromise."

"It would probably be a very moderate measure," he admitted.

"Take the question of Parliamentary reform," I continued. "Suppose the Crown and the majority of the Council to be opposed to it, and a bill to be brought in and carried in the Commons. The Lords might reject it, and the Crown refuse to overcome their opposition by creating new peers; or they might pass it, and the Crown interpose its veto. The result would be a revolution."

"Just so," he rejoined. "In such a case, we admit the sacred right of insurrection."

"Your ideal perfect system of government, then, is an absolute monarchy, tempered by impeachments and revolutions," I said.

"Do you forget that the Commons have the power of stopping the supplies?" he asked.

"Oh no," I replied. "But the consequences of such a step on their part would be the downfall of the monarchy. Every department of the State would be thrown into anarchy and confusion. The clerks would leave their stools, there would be no postal service, the army would be disbanded, our ships would be without seamen, and no sound of adze or hammer would be heard in the dockyards. Then the Republicans would be at work, asking the people whether monarchy was worth preserving at such a price; and we should have a revolution as surely as we should if the Commons had not the power of refusing supplies."

There the conversation dropped, for neither of us was likely to be convinced by the arguments of the other.

Have I exaggerated the probable result of the system which Urquhart advocated? It was possible only while the Constitution existed only in theory, and the House of Commons submitted to be told, as it was by Elizabeth, that its function was to vote supplies, that its duty was to vote such as were asked for, and that it should not meddle in the affairs of the State. That system was shaken under the first of the Stuarts, and broke down, dragging the monarchy with it, under his successor.

CHAPTER XIX.

THE STORY OF THE HYDE PARK RAILINGS.

WHILE the question of Parliamentary reform was occupying men's minds in this country, almost to the exclusion of every other topic, events were in progress on the continent of Europe which both my professional duties and my political sympathies caused me to watch with great attention. I had studied, through all its phases, the question out of which they arose, and which every journalist was expected to write about, and did write about, whether he understood it or not; and the Dano-German war of 1865 had invested it with a degree of interest for me which it had never had before.

My acquaintance with the interminable Schleswig-Holstein question had commenced nearly twenty years previously, when I learned the views of the German Liberals concerning it through my connexion with the Fraternal Democrats. There was not a member of the German section of that association who did not regard the Elbe duchies as naturally forming a part of the Germany of the future; but the question was not regarded from the same point of view in Downing Street and in Drury Lane. The diplomatists made a much more tangled skein of it; and it was impossible for me, as a journalist, to ignore their views and conclusions, though the problem involved in them was decidedly of a brain-turning tendency.

"This grows interesting," I said to my colleague, when the news came of Prussia's secession from the Bund. "This act of the Prussian Government raises a question far larger than that of the Danish succession and the shadowy claims of Russia."

"Nothing will come of it," rejoined my colleague. "The Prussian Ministers are puppets moved by wires pulled by Prince Gortschakoff. The Bund may be broken, but there will be only another shuffling of the cards by hands bound to play the game of Russia."

"I credit Count Bismarck with more patriotism than the German sovereigns have ever shown," said I, "and with foresight enough to perceive that the unity of Germany is 'looming in the future;' and, as the means by which that long-felt aspiration of the German people can be realized are limited, by the nature of the obstacles to be overcome, to war and revolution, there can be no doubt as to which King William and his ministers will choose."

"German unity is a dream," observed the London correspondent, with a yawn.

"You said that of Italian unity," I rejoined. "Two steps have been taken towards making the unity of Germany a reality already. The wresting of the Elbe duchies from Denmark was the first; the refusal of Prussia to submit to the decision of the Diet constitutes the second. The disruption of the Bund, preparatory to the formation of a new one, of which Prussia shall be the head, must follow, if the unity of Germany is to be accomplished by war, instead of by revolution."

"I think you are wrong," said the London correspondent. "Mr. Urquhart says there will be no war, and I have never found him wrong. Russia does not wish for war; and Bismarck and Beust, and the rest of them, being her tools, there will consequently be no war."

Whether Urquhart knew, or only guessed, that Russia did not wish to see hostilities between Prussia and Austria, it is probable that he was correct in his representation of the views of the Court and Cabinet of St. Petersburg at that period. That his prediction was falsified by the event was due to the fundamental error of his political creed, which attributed to the Russian Foreign Office, by whomsoever directed, an all-pervading and all-powerful influence in every Court and Cabinet, from Lisbon to Pekin. Russia had no reason to wish for war, because she had no desire either to see Prussia prostrate at the feet of Austria, or the German Bund broken up, and a new and stronger confederation erected upon its ruins.

So far Urquhart was right. But Count Bismarck was not likely to betray German interests in order to serve the aims of Russia, or of any other foreign Power; and it was by supposing the contrary that Urquhart was led into the utterance of a prediction that was not to be fulfilled.

I was assured, however, that his confident anticipation of the maintenance of peace was shared by the German merchants in Liverpool, and that only a few days before the Prussian armies poured through the defiles of the Bohemian mountains. The wish was probably father to the thought; for commercial considerations stand before all others in Liverpool, as much now as they did in the bad old slave-dealing days.

"They care for nothing but cotton," said a gentleman who was well acquainted with the Liverpudlian mind. "They would have the Queen's speech left out of the paper rather than a consular report on the capabilities of a new cotton-field."

It is not an easy task for a journalist, whatever his politics may be, to express convictions that will harmonize at all times with the tendencies of thought in Liverpool, and especially as regards foreign politics. War and revolution must not be hinted at, or announced as imminent, because such events interfere with the operations of commerce. When they occur, they must be treated with special reference to the cotton trade. The civil war in the United States was strictly *taboo* to me on that account. The Schleswig-Holstein question was one that any number of columns might have been written about; but the larger German question that grew out of it had to be touched very tenderly.

Hostilities commenced within a week after the announcement of the founder of the Foreign Affairs Committees that there would be no war, because Russia wished for peace, was communicated to me by his friend and disciple. I watched their progress with great interest, not only on account of the political questions involved, but also for their bearing on the views which I had expressed in type five years previously as to the value of fortresses for coast and frontier defence. I was anxious to see whether the Prussian generals would repeat the errors of the great Frederick a hundred years previously, and stand knocking their heads against the walls of Koniggratz and Josephstadt a longer time than it would take them to march to Vienna. The results showed that Von Moltke was a better tactician than Mr. Carlyle's hero, and that the views I had expressed when discussing the Palmerstonian project of defence were as sound as they could have been if I had studied in the best military colleges; perhaps much more so, for the reason that explains the discomfiture of a skilled fencer by one who has never handled foil or sword before.

I was soon recalled to questions of more immediate interest, however, by the agitation for Parliamentary reform, which during the autumn of 1866 began to once more assume a threatening character. The period between the resignation of the Russell-Gladstone Ministry and the opening of Parliament in the following year was one of such excitement and suspense as the nation had not known since 1848. No one could tell how far we were from the verge of revolution. We were not far from it on the evening when the Hyde Park railings were demolished. The sterling common sense of Englishmen availed, however, to avert a collision and a crash that in France would have been inevitable. Mr. Beales remonstrated with a strong force behind him; Mr. Walpole shed tears, and yielded. The police were withdrawn from a position which they could not have held long, unless supported by troops, and the mob surged triumphantly over the park.

The demolition of the Hyde Park railings has generally been ascribed to the Reformers, and there can be little doubt that it was the work of men who sympathized with them, aided by the "roughs" who assemble upon every occasion that promises riot and disorder. But there is an error in the supposition that the long breach in the railings was made by the men who marched to Hyde Park with bands and banners, with the intention of making a demonstration there in favour of Parliamentary reform.

I was on my way to the park on that eventful evening, some time before the assault on the railings, and met the procession in Grosvenor Place, marching four abreast, and in admirable order, with bands playing the quaint air known as John Brown's Hymn.

"What is up?" I asked, as I fell into the rear of the column.

"The park gates are closed," was the reply of the man I addressed.

"Where to now?" was my next question.

"Trafalgar Square," was the concise response; and on we tramped.

At the bottom of Grosvenor Place a halt was called, for the purpose of communicating the change of purpose to the marshals of another column which was there met, and enabling it to effect a junction with the one I had joined. Some obstruction to the traffic was created by this halt before we got into motion again, but, as many of the processionists fell out to obtain refreshments, and no disposition to impede traffic unnecessarily was shown, no vehicle was delayed more than a minute or two. I assisted in making a passage for more than one carriage in which there were ladies, and met with no obstruction in doing so; nor did I hear an offensive expression addressed to any one, whatever impatience was manifested by those who were impeded in their progress.

It was while the Reformers were on their way to Trafalgar Square that the sympathizers with the movement who had not joined the procession, the men and women who were on their way to the park, as on other evenings, and the " roughs " and idlers whom the throng about the park gates caused to congregate, attempted to force their way into the park, and, after several skirmishes with the police, overthrew the railings, and burst into it like a torrent.

The Derby-Disraeli Ministry saw that they must either yield to the popular pressure, expose the country to the risk of revolution, or resign. They yielded, and the result was the Representation Act of 1867, which fulfilled my prediction of thirteen years previously, that the adoption of a rating franchise would involve the repeal of the Rating Acts. The majority in the House of Commons were committed, by their votes upon Mr. Gladstone's bill, to the principle of a rating franchise, and Mr. Disraeli's bill brought the compound householder question to the front as soon as it was propounded. If a householder rated at five pounds, and paying the rates direct to the collector, was to be enfranchised, why not the occupier of a ten pound house the rates of which were included in the rent? No answer to this query could be found, and the House drifted into household suffrage as the inevitable consequence.

Another advance towards manhood suffrage and uniform electoral districts was made by this measure, proposed by a Conservative Ministry, and adopted by a reactionary House of Commons. The next step will be the assimilation of the county and borough franchises, already "looming in the future," to quote an expression of Lord Beaconsfield's many years ago, and then the carving out of the country into electoral districts of uniform pattern and equal population, on the plan laid down in the People's Charter, will become inevitable.

Always regarding political power as a means to an end, and that end the amelioration of the conditions of life, or, as Bentham expressed it, "the greatest happiness of the greatest number," I expected much from the Act of 1867, followed as it was next year by the return to office, and for the first time as First Minister of the Crown, of Mr.

Gladstone. I need scarcely say that I was disappointed. Mr. Gladstone either failed to comprehend the requirements of the new situation created by the "leap in the dark" of his predecessors in office, or he could not resolve at the right moment to adopt the only course by which his popularity could be maintained. He made, in some instances, a bad selection of colleagues, notably in the case of Mr. Lowe, who had not only done everything in his power to prevent that enfranchisement of the people which had made the Gladstone Ministry a necessity, but had grievously insulted the working classes during the debate on Mr. Disraeli's bill by the assertion that every man might have a vote if he would live in a decent house instead of squandering his wages upon gin and beer.

But the popular Premier's mistakes were not confined to the original one of a bad choice of colleagues. The true policy, since 1867, for any Ministry, whether called Liberal or Conservative, was, and is, the amelioration of the laws affecting the working classes by the removal of the blots which the toiling millions naturally regarded as the consequences of their exclusion from political power. But Mr. Gladstone failed to perceive this. The one-sidedness of the law of employer and employed was left to be partially amended by a Conservative Ministry. The removal of one of the blackest blots in the law of landlord, tenant, and lodger was not effected by a Ministerial measure, but was due to the independent action of Lord Shaftesbury. The law of husband and wife, which has been amended by wrong-headed philanthropists in the interests of the so-called weaker vessel until it has become a source of monstrous injustice to the natural head of the family—the law of divorce, from the benefit of which the working classes, who most need it, are practically excluded—these were left untouched, and remain a source of constant irritation and growing discontent.

While I was watching, with a growing feeling of disappointment, the course pursued by Mr. Gladstone on his return to office with advantages on his side which he had never possessed before, my attention was drawn to the under-currents of foreign politics by the discovery of a mysterious connexion between Urquhart and the ultramontane Romanists. I had never met the former, and knew him only by repute as the persistent denouncer of Palmerston and promulgator of the idea that the Ministers of the State should be merely the private secretaries of the Sovereign, the inevitable tendency of that system to despotism being corrected by the power of impeaching and beheading Privy Councillors who gave the Sovereign unconstitutional advice, and the right of rebelling against Sovereigns who refused to be guided by advice in accordance with the Constitution.

In 1868 I did not know whether Urquhart was a Protestant or a Romanist, a Voltairean or a Mussulman, though his admiration of everything Turkish had at one time led me to suspect that his mind had received a Mohammedan tinge during his residence at Constantinople and his travels through Ottoman territories. But when I saw the pages of the *Diplomatic Review* filled, month after month, with abuse of every political celebrity who was not either a Romanist or a Turk, mingled with extravagant eulogy of the Pope and mysterious references to some council that was to settle all the outstanding questions of the day, I could not avoid the conclusion that the writer must be either a Romanist or a rival of the eccentric Ackerly.[1]

That he was not a Romanist I was assured by a journalist who was both a member of that communion and his friend and disciple. But I was not long in discovering that the Council was the Œcumenical,

---

[1] The present generation may require to be informed that Ackerly was an eccentric naval lieutenant who claimed to have invented a wonderful lamp, which possessed the property of curing all diseases, and was named by him the " Lamp of Life.' He sometimes made an appearance on the platform at political meetings, whence he spoke for a few minutes on the question of the occasion, but invariably strayed from it to the " Lamp of Life." Mysterious advertisements in cipher were occasionally inserted by him in the evening journals, these also referring, as far as they were intelligible, to his alleged discovery.

from which so much was expected at that time by the friends of the Papacy. My attention was directed by the discovery to the proceedings of that assembly, the objects of which were declared, by the bull convening it, to be the securing of the integrity of the Catholic faith, the enforcement of respect for religion and the ecclesiastical laws, the improvement of public morals, the establishment of peace and concord, and the removal of all the evils that afflict society. Grand aims were some of these, and worthy of the support of all good men; but the true meaning of the language in which they were announced could be read between the lines.

The Council met towards the close of the following year. What was the product of its labours? Did it improve public morals, establish peace and concord, and remove all the evils that afflict society? Did it accomplish any one of those objects, or even propound any feasible plan for its realization? On the contrary, its sole outcome was the doctrine of Papal infallibility, the promulgation of which brought about the Old Catholic schism in Germany, and was followed, immediately after the rising of the Council, by a decree of the Vatican which was at once a challenge and a menace. The Papal bull *Latæ sententiæ* was a spiritual lasso cast about the throat of every Catholic, who found himself thenceforward unable to read any book, the perusal of which was forbidden by the Pope, or to question any utterance of the Vatican oracle upon any subject, without rendering himself liable to excommunication.

Three or four years afterwards, when the struggle between the Romish clergy and the State reached Switzerland, and caused dissension and strife at Berne and Geneva, an appeal was addressed by the former to foreign Catholic Powers in terms which brought it under the notice of the Federal Government. Urquhart, who was then residing at Geneva, and the Abbé Collet, an ultramontane French priest, also staying in that city, were arrested on suspicion of being the authors and promulgators of the appeal, whereupon the Abbé Defourny, who had taken care by remaining at Beaumont not to put himself within the reach of the Swiss police, addressed a letter to the President of the Republic, acknowledging that he was the author of the document. Urquhart was discharged; but the Abbé Collet, who was proved to have circulated the appeal from Geneva, was expelled forthwith from Swiss territory.

The Protestantism of David Urquhart (if he was a Protestant) must have been of a very peculiar type. It never prompted him to advocate the cause of Protestantism, or of a Protestant State. Those who came under his ban were invariably Protestants, or Catholics whom the priests would not acknowledge as being within the fold of the Romish Church.

CHAPTER XX.

THE POPULAR LITERATURE OF THE PRESENT DAY.

During a temporary cessation of my journalistic occupations, I renewed my connexion with the periodical press, as a contributor of stories of adventure to publications circulating very extensively among boys and young men, and subsequently continued it for a time as the editor of one of them. A great improvement had been effected in this department of our most popular literature during the interval which had elapsed since my former connexion with it. The enormous multiplication of readers, and the success which had rewarded the publishers who enlisted in their services such writers of fiction as Miss Braddon and Mr. W. H. Ainsworth, had given the incentive, at the same time that they increased the profits of the proprietors and raised the rate of remuneration to authors.

The obscure writers for the preceding generation had been succeeded, as contributors of fiction to the penny periodicals, by the authors just named, and by

Thomas Miller, one of the best descriptive poets of the age, as well as a novelist of more than average ability; Watts Phillips, the dramatist; Captain Mayne Reid, whose exciting stories of life and adventure among the wild tribes of the American prairies are read by boys with such avidity; Mr. Percy St. John and Mr. Vane St. John, brothers of the author of "Purple Tints of Paris;" Mr. Edmund Yates, the author of numerous novels to be found on the shelves of Mudie's library; Mr. James Greenwood, the author of "Low Life Deeps," who had achieved a peculiar distinction a few years previously by undergoing the ordeal of a night in the casual ward of Lambeth workhouse, in order to qualify himself to relate his experiences in the columns of an evening journal; Townsend, the veteran dramatist; Mr. Charles H. Ross, editor of *Judy*; and, last, though not least in repute or talent Mr. G. A. Sala.

Townsend and Hildyard, both deceased, the two St. Johns, Mr. Greenwood, and Mr. Ross, were among the contributors of serial stories to the publications with which I was connected at the period referred to in the beginning of this chapter. The literary quality of the stories was very much superior to that of the fictions issued forty years ago, though the latter were read more by adults than by boys, and the former were written especially for the hundreds of thousands of boy readers whom the increased diffusion of a taste for reading had called into existence during the interval. Without any lowering of the moral tone, they presented more faithful transcripts of real life; while they avoided equally the sensualism of the school of Eugène Sue, and the mawkish sentimentality of the Minerva library novels of our fathers' days, they abounded in the sensational element.

Persons who regard the reading of even the best works of fiction as at the least a waste of time that might be better employed seem to regard sensational incidents as peculiar to what they call "penny dreadfuls," and even many novel readers have a vague belief in the existence of a sensational school of fiction, of which they regard Miss Braddon as the founder. Perhaps they have not read Godwin's novels, or the romances of Anne Radcliffe; or, to go back to the early years of the English novel, Smollett's "Count Fathom," a perusal of which would convince any reader that the introduction of the sensational element did not await Miss Braddon. No chapter of modern fiction is more sensational than Smollett's description of the storm in the forest, which Ferdinand takes shelter from in the hut of a gang of robbers, and finds the still warm corpse of one of their victims concealed beneath some straw; the placing of the corpse in his own bed, which saves his life, and his escape from the hut, guided by an old hag whom he compels to accompany him through the forest.

What, too—coming down to a later date than Smollett's time, or even Godwin's, and yet before the publication of "Lady Audley's Secret"—what of Mr. W. Harrison Ainsworth's romances? of "Rookwood," "Guy Fawkes," and "Old St. Paul's"? What of Lord Lytton's "Paul Clifford," "Eugene Aram," "Lucretia," and that splendid creation of genius, "The Last Days of Pompeii"? There are few novels worth reading, indeed, that are devoid of sensation; both because the quality of a work of fiction must be tested by its fidelity to real life, and there are few lives that are unmarked by some sensational incident; and because the genius that can evoke interest out of lives that have been from birth to death unmarked by anything more exciting than the first throb of the tender passion is of the rarest order.

That there is a larger amount of the sensational element in the fiction of the last fifty years than in the novels of any earlier period is, however, indisputable; and one of the causes is so intimately connected with the periodical form of publication that it ought not to be passed over. Writers of fiction for magazines are placed at a disadvantage, compared with those whose works are issued complete, in two or three volumes, in having their work judged by its monthly instalments; and this remark applies, as a matter of course, with fourfold force to those whose stories appear at weekly intervals, and in much smaller instalments, in the columns of a periodical. They are compelled, by the requirements of that mode of publication, to work up the interest to as high a pitch as possible at the close of each instalment, and to keep the reader's curiosity ungratified until the appearance of the next, or a later one. This can be accomplished only by creating a succession of sensational incidents and effective situations. Two or three numbers consecutively without excitement, whatever might be the author's talent in the description of scenery or the delineation (as apart from the development) of character, would ruin the sale of the work, and damage the writer's reputation both with the publisher and the public. The fictionist who writes for a periodical requires, therefore, a greater power of working up to dramatic situations, as well as a larger share of constructive skill, than one who believes only in three-volumed novels at a guinea and a half, and depends upon the circulating libraries.

When Mr. Wilkie Collins, more than twenty years ago, announced his discovery, somewhat late, of "a reading public of three millions which lies right out of the pale of literary civilization," drawing, in so doing, a not very obvious distinction between twopenny and penny publications, he expressed the opinion that the existing generation of readers of the latter were unable to distinguish between good and bad stories, using the adjectives with reference to their literary merits, and not to their moral tone; at the same time coupling with it his conviction that "the very best men among living English writers will one of these days be called on, as a matter of necessity, to make their appearance in the pages of the penny journals. Meanwhile," he added, "it is perhaps hardly too much to say that the future of English fiction may rest with this Unknown Public, which is now waiting to be taught the difference between a good book and a bad. It is probably a question of time only. The largest audience for periodical literature, in this age of periodicals, must obey the universal law of progress, and must, sooner or later, learn to discriminate. When that period comes, the readers who rank by millions will be the readers who give the widest reputations, who return the richest rewards, and will therefore command the services of the best writers of their time. A great, an unparalleled prospect awaits, perhaps, the coming generation of English novelists. To the penny journals of the present time belongs the credit of having discovered a new public. When that public shall discover its need of a great writer, the great writer will have such an audience as has never yet been known."

With regard to the strictures of Mr. Wilkie Collins on the literary taste of the masses, the truth seems to be that, while the very highest order of genius is appreciated only by a comparatively small number of readers, the authors whose works are most in request among the subscribers to Mudie's are also those which stand highest in the favour of the readers of penny periodicals, so far at least as they have been brought within their reach. Education makes a considerable difference, not only in the preference of one author to another, but in the preference of one work to another of the same author. Thus, the under-current of metaphysics in some of Lord Lytton's novels, the knowledge of history which is necessary to the complete appreciation of his historical romances, make him a greater favourite with the cultured few than with the many. Even among the educated "Ernest Maltravers" is, as a rule, preferred to "Rienzi" and "The Last Days of Pompeii." The masses who were reading the "Dick Turpin" and "Jerry Abershaw" of Mr. Miles when the educated classes were revelling in Mr. Ainsworth's "Rookwood" and "Jack Sheppard," and Lord Lytton's "Paul Clifford," now prefer one of Dickens's stories. Yet Dickens, in his own walk, was as great a genius as Lord Lytton.

Theirs are the only two names which can be placed in the first rank among writers of the generation that is passing away; and they are the two whose works have been most frequently reprinted, in every form, even to numbers at three-halfpence, and, therefore, the most extensively read by all classes. Until another Dickens or another Lytton arises, and writes for a penny periodical, who can say that the best works of fiction are not appreciated by the millions?

It is very doubtful whether authors of the stamp of Lord Lytton and Charles Dickens will be more numerous in the next generation than in the present, but there will be no lack of writers of the moderate amount of literary ability, which, combined with adequate knowledge of the world, suffices for the production of an interesting story. The literary class multiplies in the ratio of the increase of readers, though the proportion of authors who obtain a hearing to the aspirants who fail is very small. Those who have had no experience of editorial duties would be surprised to find how large is the number of persons who aspire to a literary status, and imagine that they possess the necessary qualifications. Still more surprised would they be to find that the majority of the young persons who are attacked with the *cacoethes scribendi* entertain the delusion that they are qualified to shine in the departments of fiction and poetry.

The manuscripts submitted to me during my year's experience as the editor of a penny periodical consisted almost entirely of stories and poetry, or rather verses. The writers were, as a rule, unknown to fame, and a large proportion of them were not merely unpractised in authorcraft, but had not even cultivated the essential studies of grammar and composition. A short story, the writer of which had not attempted to depict phases of life with which he was unacquainted, or a little poem which did not take too lofty a flight, could sometimes be selected from a pile of manuscripts; but the majority had to be rejected. As the longer stories were calculated to run through a dozen or fifteen numbers of the periodical, the reading of them would have been a terrible infliction if a large proportion had not betrayed, in the first or second chapter, an amount of incapacity for novel-writing sufficient to preclude the necessity of reading the remainder. I never rejected a manuscript on the ground of its being avowedly a first attempt, or because the writer was unknown; but inexperience was generally the least fault exhibited by the stories which were submitted to me. Impossible incidents, colourless or conventional characters, vapid or extravagant dialogue, often marred stories that indicated some idea of the manner in which a story should be told, and did not offend very seriously on the score of grammar and style; and, as a rule, incapacity to construct a natural plot and develope character in a life-like manner was greater in the same proportion as the story was longer and more pretentious.

Editors would be spared much trouble, and aspirants to record on the muster-roll of fame much disappointment, if those who aim at the honours of type in the department of fiction could be convinced that there is much that is essential to success, besides the desire to write a story, and the fancy that they are capacitated to produce one that will not carry its condemnation on its face. The would-be novelist must first learn to write grammatically, and to express his ideas intelligibly upon paper; and when these acquirements have been mastered, he or she would do well to go through a course of reading, not necessarily of works of fiction (which it would perhaps be best to avoid), but of the best productions of the great masters of English composition. Having thus prepared himself, the aspirant may attempt a story, though it is very unlikely, unless he possesses qualifications for the task far above the average, that his first production will ever be printed; unless, indeed, he should achieve a name by subsequent stories, and be so unconscientious as to publish such a crudity on the strength thereof, and be rendered callous to criticism by the knowledge that his repute will carry to the libraries any rubbish that bears his name on the title-page.

His chances of success will be greatly improved, however, if he refrains from attempting to depict phases of life with which he has no acquaintance, and resolutely abjures conventional types of character. Many a story that might have been pronounced fairly good if the author had adopted this rule is marred by its neglect, which invariably stamps it with an air of unreality. The portrayal of character requires the development of the faculties of observation and delineation in a degree that is rare even among experienced fictionists; but embryo novelists would avoid those absurdities which editors are often asked to accept as representations of modern life and manners, if they would aim at depicting only the section or sections of humanity with which they are best acquainted. The man or woman who can write tolerable English may, by observing this precaution, produce a story that may be deemed worthy of acceptance, and even achieve a fair degree of success; while its neglect may cause the manuscript to be laid aside on the perusal of a chapter or two, because the author betrays ignorance of the manners and language of the classes or vocations from which he has selected his characters.

If the poetry, or rather the verses which the writers supposed to be poetry, tried my patience less than the crude efforts of would-be novelists, it was only because the task of reading was sooner got through. A score of songs, odes, and sonnets could be read in a comparatively short time, even when the caligraphy was feminine. But, oh! the bad rhymes, the defective metres, the sacrifices of sense to sound, the absence of anything in the language or the ideas to atone for such faults! I sometimes mended both rhyme and metre, when a poem was a little above the average in other respects; but such rhymes as "mine" and "time," which represent one of the most frequent faults of that kind, would be corrected in vain when there is not a poetic idea, or the smallest grace of language, in the verses which they help to disfigure.

The correspondence column of a popular periodical is, perhaps, more amusing to the editor than to the reader, who, however, may derive instruction from the perusal, though he may not find it very entertaining. The questions addressed to the editor of a periodical are multifarious, and all the works of reference on his shelves, or in the reading-room of the Museum, will not always enable him to answer them. He will be asked, for instance, how to train a dog, without being told what the animal is to be trained for; what the cost of binding a volume of the periodical will be, without any style being specified; what he thinks of the writer's handwriting, the letter looking as if it had been carefully written at the commencement, and finished in a hurry; which of two specimens of caligraphy is the best, the two being so much alike that they appear to have been written by the same hand; which is the best colony to emigrate to, no information being given as to the writer's occupation, means, or pursuits; and many equally varied questions, with the like absence of the information without which they cannot be answered.

Some of the letters received from boys are rather amusing. "Sur," writes one, who was supposed to be a machine-boy, upon the circumstantial evidence afforded by the impression on the envelope of a finger soiled with printing-ink. "I wont to be a midshipman, but I dont no how to git apinted. Will you plese tell me in yure next wot I must do. I ham neerly fifteen, and no a little of sea life, as I have red lots of nortical tales."

"Dear sir," writes another, in the plain, bold caligraphy of a schoolboy, "can you tell me why apples make me red in the face when I eat them? I am very fond of apples, especially Ribstone pippins, but when I eat many I get red in the face directly, and feel hot and uncomfortable."

"Sir," says a third, whose education seems to have been no better cared for than that of the would-be midshipman, "Plese tell me what you think of the enclosed play, wich I have rote all myself. I think it ort to be sensayshunal enuf for anythink, and if you think its propper, plese send it to any theayter were you nose the guvner, and have it brought hout. You mite say that all the boys at hour shop will go and see it." This last epistle accompanied the manuscript of a drama of the most original and extraordinary character—a melodrama of the old Adelphi school, and certainly fulfilling the writer's description of it as " sensayshunal enuf for anythink."

Many correspondents write only to express their approval or otherwise of the current serial stories, and I once received a communication to the following effect, written upon a dirty quarter sheet of post:— " Mr. Editor,—If you dont give us a good highwayman story, we shant take your pub. any longer. So take notis. JACK SHEPPARD, DICK TURPIN, TOM KING, CLAUDE DUVAL, JACK RANN, JEM DALTON, JOE BLAKE, PAUL CLIFFORD, TOM RAIN." The young gentlemen who had signed this collective missive, probably a knot of machine-boys at some neighbouring printing-office, were informed that their wishes could not be complied with, and received at the same time a friendly warning, founded upon the names they had assumed, which, it may be hoped, has not been without its intended influence upon their lives.

CHAPTER XXI.

THE FALL OF THE GLADSTONE MINISTRY.

During the time that I combined the occupation of a contributor to periodicals with the task of writing articles upon political and social questions for provincial newspapers, I had little difficulty in shaping my journalistic course so as to express my convictions without clashing with the views or offending the susceptibilities of the moderate Liberals, as the Gladstone Ministry was as far from being satisfactory to the Whigs as it was to the Radicals. It is a curious fact, indeed, that I was more uniformly successful in writing for a Whig journal, as the Shrewsbury paper was, than in the articles written for the Liverpudlian organ of independent Liberalism. The cause seemed to be that the principles of the former were more distinctly defined than those of the latter, which were liable to modification from local and personal influences.

There came a time, however, when an important section of my Salopian readers questioned the soundness of my arguments and rejected my counsel. The movement of the agricultural labourers for an advance of wages was at that time fluttering the minds of the farmers, some of whom (the wish being father to the thought,) consoled themselves with the reflection that it would result in failure, while the more thoughtful among them remembered my prophecy on the subject, and shook their heads.

Years before the farm labourers' unions were formed, or the name of Joseph Arch had been heard, I had told the farmers of Shropshire that the time was near when their labourers would follow the example of the workmen in towns, and organize themselves for the promotion of the interests, or what they might conceive to be the interests, of their class. The prediction had now been fulfilled, and the farmers were face to face with a difficulty which their fathers had never experienced, or even contemplated as possible.

When strikes began to occur, and the farmers were suffering inconvenience from the suspension of agricultural labour, I endeavoured to remove from their minds the fallacy that the relations between capital and labour are different in the case of agriculture from those existing in the case of manufactures. I argued that the position of the farm labourer, with regard to the wages question, was precisely the same as that of the urban artisan or factory operative, and that the issue would be determined by the same conditions. If the labourers were demanding higher wages than the state of the labour-market justified, their movement would fail; but if the farmers could not replace the men on strike by equally competent labourers at the existing rates of wages, the rise would have to be conceded.

The soundness of this reasoning would have been recognized at once by London builders or Lancashire cotton-spinners; but the argument was new to the farmers of Shropshire, and it equally surprised and angered them. At a meeting held at the Raven Hotel, Shrewsbury, in March, 1872, my views were severely criticized by some of the bucolic speakers, and the politico-economical grounds on which they were based were questioned as broadly as they had ever been by workmen in the early days of trades unionism, when workmen were much less intelligent and more imperfectly educated than those of the present generation. The farmers could not see their way to any increase of wages unless the owners of the land would consent to recoup them by accepting reduced rents; and rent, I had told them, was as much a question of supply and demand as labour.

I had warned them that, if the labourers' movement failed, there were men among them intelligent enough to discover the cause, and that discovered, they would prepare for a renewal of the struggle by organizing an extensive emigration. If it succeeded, whether then or later, and the farmers quitted their farms, as they had stated they must do in that event, the rent of land would be lowered through the diminution of the demand for farms; but they must not expect any reduction of rent, whatever rate of wages they might have to pay, while the demand for farms remained undiminished.

As the effervescence subsided, I availed of such opportunities as were afforded by new applications of steam to agricultural purposes, or the expression of large views by eminent agriculturists, to draw the attention of the farmers to the new conditions which steam cultivation was introducing into agriculture, and to advocate co-operative farming as the only means by which, with advanced rates of wages and the augmented value of land, farmers of small capital could compete successfully with their richer neighbours. But the fruits of the suggestion are as yet indiscernible.

The Gladstone Ministry, from which so much had been expected by the working classes, was, in the meantime, tottering to its fall. The Education Act having, to some extent, disappointed the expectations of the people, both by its permissive character and by the inapplicability of its provisions to districts where they were most needed, what was there in the other measures of Mr. Gladstone to compensate for its shortcomings? From the point of view of the newly enfranchised working man—who, as well as his father before him, had been for years waiting for the result of Parliamentary reform in the amelioration of the laws which injuriously affected the moral and material welfare of their class—*nothing*.

That is the true solution of the waning of Mr. Gladstone's popularity and the recovered ascendancy of the Conservatives, who, under the educative process of Mr. Disraeli, had shown themselves so pliable, that working men, caring nothing for party, did not hesitate to throw the weight of their numbers into the same scale with the Tory-Radical statesman's genius and Lord Derby's sound common sense. Mr. Gladstone showed himself as unable to understand that his popularity was diminishing as he had been to perceive the necessity of surrounding himself with Radical colleagues, and introducing measures for the amelioration of the laws affecting the working classes, when political power had been given to the masses by the Act of 1867. While the Parks Bill and Ballot Bill were in progress, and when it was rumoured that Parliament would be dissolved as soon as they had been passed, Mr. Monk took occasion to note the increasing divergence of the Government from the views of their supporters.

"I certainly think," he observed, "that their policy has not been very successful; in fact, the results of recent elections show how far it has succeeded. They have not gained, but have lost several able men since the last general election; and, unless they turn their attention to more important measures, which are less obnoxious to the country,[1] I am afraid that, when the next general election takes place, not even the Ballot Bill will save them from the disagreeable necessity of crossing to the other side of the House."

How much this apprehension coincided with the popular feeling on the subject of the Gladstonian policy was soon afterwards demonstrated; but the Premier viewed the consequences of the divergence commented upon by Mr. Monk with as light a heart as M. Ollivier carried with regard to that fatal march Rhineward which was to have terminated at Berlin, but was rolled back with crushing disaster upon Paris. "Some of the questions raised by the honourable member for Gloucester," he observed, with irony so marked that it occasioned a laugh, "are really of great magnitude, and such as I hardly feel myself in a position to enter into a discussion upon at this moment."

I have quoted from Mr. Monk's speech and Mr. Gladstone's reply because I made them the text of an article written for my Liverpool readers, but excluded by the pressure of local and commercial matter, from which I extract a few passages to show

---

[1] Referring to the Parks Bill.

how the situation was regarded by me, and I believe by the majority of the nation.

"The remarks made by the honourable member for Gloucester," I wrote, "represent so truthfully the actual state of the case that the manner of their reception by the Premier cannot have failed to make an impression upon the public mind most detrimental to the right honourable gentleman's position. It is so incredible that Mr. Gladstone should be ignorant of the nature of the measures expected from a Liberal Ministry, as the natural result of the measures which he and his supporters assisted the Derby-Disraeli Administration to pass in 1867, that the working classes may be excused if they regard him as a statesman who, having succeeded in reaching the highest position under the Crown by popular aid, is now disposed to kick over the ladder by which he has mounted. These classes now form so large a proportion of the constituencies that the existence of such a feeling on their part would justify the warning of Mr. Monk, while the manner in which the warning was received must cause the political prospect to be regarded by men of moderate views with no small degree of anxiety."

After referring to the rumour of a dissolution as soon as the Ballot Bill had become law, I went on to observe that "the disappointment which has been suffered by the working-classes, and which manifests itself more plainly every day, may help to give a numerical preponderance to the Conservatives in the next House of Commons; but such a result, unless in the improbable event of Mr. Disraeli being not only better disposed than Mr. Gladstone to propose the ameliorative measures which have been expected, but also to 'educate' his followers to the point of accepting them, would tend only to hasten that disruption and reconstitution of parties which is 'looming in the future.'

"Before many years have passed, we shall probably see many ranged under the Conservative banner who now support Mr. Gladstone, while the opposite side of the House will be occupied by a new Liberal party, acknowledging another chief than Mr. Gladstone, unless he should find reason to amend his view of the situation. Who the leader will be, and what the extent of the changes demanded, if the masses should be urged by Ministerial neglect into the exertion of all the resources of industrial organization for the purpose of creating a new party in the House of Commons, are questions which cannot be answered, whatever the anxiety with which they may well be regarded."

These passages throw some light upon the causes of Mr. Gladstone's rapid decline in popularity after attaining the Premiership, and the restoration of the Conservatives to power by the largest vote ever recorded, except in 1868. It was not so much by the estrangement of the religious profession by the Education Act, or of the beer trade by the Licensing Act, that the Gladstone Ministry fell, as by the inclusion of Mr. Lowe in the Cabinet and the neglect of those social questions the solution of which had been regarded by two generations of working men as the first fruits of the attainment of political power by their class.

In looking back upon the period covered by these recollections of an active life, and comparing the present with the past, the progress which has been achieved during that time in all that tends to the moral and intellectual dignity of humanity is so great, that I should be deemed the dreamer I was thought to be forty years ago if I attempted to depict the probable state of the world, political and social, even a quarter of a century hence. When I consider the rapidly developing intellect of the nations that are foremost in civilization, the amount of political power already possessed by them, and the unrivalled capacity for organization of the Teutonic race in particular, I cannot doubt that the future of those nations is in their own hands, or that, though there may be some mistakes and failures by the way, they will so mould the future structure of society, that the Europe of 1900 will exceed, in all that makes the true greatness of nations, the Europe of to-day even more than that which we now see excels the condition of the same nations half a century ago.

The true greatness of a nation must be measured by the condition of the masses. Rome fell because the masses of the Empire were poor, ignorant, enslaved. This standard will be more and more the criterion of national power and influence as the working classes advance in education, sobriety, and union. Those classes everywhere constitute the majority of the population, and the ratio of their numbers to those of the distributing and other non-producing classes will continually increase as the progress of the co-operative movement, and the constant tendency to employ larger capitals in business, gradually diminish the number of the small shopkeepers, always the least progressive portion of the community.

The increased power of the masses will constitute the best guarantee for the maintenance of peace between nations, so essential to their progress, by uniting the working men of all countries in a great league of universal brotherhood, which will render it impossible for rulers to array one nation against another for the gratification of their own ambition or territorial greed. The *vox populi* will be heard in louder tones year by year as the badge of political inferiority is worn by fewer and fewer of the people, as education becomes more widely diffused, and the intellectual powers more fully developed. It will be heard more frequently and potentially in the House of Commons, and then there will be an end of the fallacies which now escape detection, and the blunders that are made and listened to with as much gravity as if they were the utterances of an oracle, whenever questions affecting the moral or material interests of the masses come under legislative consideration.

Legislators, from whatever class selected, will have forced upon them the necessity of acting in accordance with the views and wishes of their constituents, or of resigning their seats when they cannot conscientiously do so; and the result will be those ameliorations of the laws which are requisite for the moral and material well-being of the people, and which have hitherto been neglected by Parliaments composed of men who neither understand the requirements of the people, nor appreciate rightly their own position as representatives. When that time comes—may it come soon!—the world will understand all that was involved in the watchword of the more intelligent and thoughtful of the working classes at the time from which the earliest of these recollections dates:—"The Charter is the means; social happiness the end."

INDEX.

ERLY, Lieut., and the Lamp of ife, 314.

llamites, origin of the party rm, 294.

-Corn Law League and the hartists, 26.

LEY, James Napier, the Socialist cturer, 16.

mby, John Goodwyn, founder of e Communist Church, 54.

iowski, Major, and the Chartists,)9.

nal Green, mission work in, 210.

kaby, James, the shoemaker- et, 30, 121, 141, 166.

ht, Mr., on the franchise ques- on, 273.

—— on the church-rate question, 30.

dett, Sir Francis, and the O'Con- ors, 171.

sey, Peter, one of the conspira- ors of 1839, 112.

[PBELL, Colin Murray, a Con- ordist, 46.

Cardo, one of the conspirators of 1839, 109.

Cassell, John, the publisher, 226.

Caxton communitorium, an unrealized project, 64.

Chambers, William and Robert, publishers, 195.

Charter Association founded, 101; new organization adopted, 143.

Charter-Socialists, views of the, 40.

Chartist conspiracy of 1848, 143.

——— demonstration on Kennington Common, 135.

——— meetings, how reported by opponents, 120.

——— movement, origin of the, 96.

Chartists, the, and the Anti-Corn-Law League, 26.

Christian Socialists, origin and views of, 40.

Chicory, extraordinary transaction in, 286.

Cleave, John, politician and publisher, 83.

Cobden, Richard, and the shoemaker, 36.

Communist Church, organization of the, 54.

——— propaganda in England, 53.

Communist periodicals forty years ago, 55, 72.
Communitive experiments in England, 21, 50, 56.
Concordist community at Ham Common, 41.
Concordium, a visit to the, 44.
Conspiracy Bill, Lord Palmerston and the, 269.
Cousins, Benjamin, and the *Penny Satirist*, 84.
Croydon fifty years ago, 2.
Cuffay, William, one of the conspirators of 1848, 149, 162.

DEFOURNY, Abbé, on the conspiracy of 1839, 105.
Denvil, Mrs., widow of the tragedian, 86.
Disraeli, Mr., on the church-rate question, 279.
Drummond, Henry, and the volunteer movement, 277.
Duncan, James Elmslie, the Socialist poet, 49.
Duncombe, Mr. T. H., in error concerning the Kennington Common demonstration, 138.

EASTHOPE, Sir John, and Feargus O'Connor, 176.
Egan, Pierce, the novelist, 86.
Elliott, Ebenezer, the Corn-Law Rhymer, 100.
Etzler's communitive paradise, 55.

FALL of the Gladstone Ministry, 334.

Farm labourers' unions and st[rikes], 332.
Finance, a curious chapter in, 2[ ]
Fleming, George Alfred, journ[alist], 183.
Fraternal Democrats, organiz[ation] of the, 125.
Fraternization of Chartists [with] foreign refugees, 129.
French spies in London, 271.
—— invasion, scare of a, 27[6]
Friswell, James Hain, a note [from] 234.
Frost, John, and the conspira[cy of] 1839, 115.
Fussell, John, the Chartist agit[ator], 146.

GALPIN, William, a vegetarian [so]cialist, 47.
Geography, official ignorance of,
Gladstone, Mr., on the church [rate] question, 279; his Reform [Bill,] 293; his failure as Premier, 334.
Greaves, James Pierrepont, [a] psychological mystic, 41.
Grosvenor, Lord Robert, and [the] Sunday Bill, 257.

HARMONY Hall, socialist experi[ment] at, 18.
Harney, George Julian, journ[alist,] 102, 183.
Hill, James, a co-operative ex[peri]mentalist, 63.
Hume, Joseph, denounced as [a re]actionist, 209.

it, Stephen, reporter and novelist, 7.
le Park railings, story of the,)3, 308.
—— Sunday riots in, 256.

LIAN refugees in London, 125, 54.

ES, Anna Maria, the novelist, 86.
—— Ernest Charles, poet and urnalist, 151, 183.

GSLEY, Charles, and the Chartst petition, 130.

DRIDGE, James, an unknown ovelist, 87.
rary institutions at Croydon, 97.
le Bentley community, in Hants, 7, 54.
yd, Mr., and the Salisbury Square ress, 84.
ett, William, author of the eople's Charter, 98.
rery, a Chartist conspirator, 111.
raft, Mr., on the paper duty uestion, 278.
telton, Lord, and the volunteer ovement, 277.

DOUALL, Dr., his escape from hester Castle, 145.
manus, Terence Bellew, an emisry of Young Ireland, 148.

Meteyard, Eliza, anecdote of, 235.
Miles, Mr. H. D., journalist and novelist, 86.
Mission work in Bethnal Green, 210.
Monk, Mr., on Mr. Gladstone's position in 1874, 335.
Moreville communitorium, Hanwell, 56.
Mullins, the Home Office spy, hanged for murder, 167.

NAPOLEON III., unrecorded incident of his visit to London, 262.
National Convention of 1839, 101.
Night march of Chartists, 145.
Noah's ark, curious discussion concerning, 217.

OASTLER, Richard, not a Chartist, 114.
Oborski, Colonel, a veteran revolutionist, 128.
O'Connor, Feargus, his account of the conspiracy of 1839, 112; at Kennington Common, 137; his early life in Ireland, 169; alleged connexion with the White Boys, 173; life in York Castle, 178; last years, 182.
Oldham, William, the Concordist, 41.
Orange Tree, arrests at the, 163.
Owen, Robert, his personal appearance, 14; libels upon, 18; founder of infant schools, 24.
Owenian Socialist movement, 13.

PAGE, David, correspondence with, 186, 193.

Palmerston, Lord, reported death of, 268; his Conspiracy Bill, 269; last years of his dictatorship, 275; his death, 289.
Paper duties, repeal of the, 277.
Parliamentary Reform Association, 203; proposal to stir up rural districts, 205; conference in St. Martin's Hall, 208.
Peel, Sir Robert, at St. Martin's Hall, 247.
People's Charter, its origin, 98.
Petition, the great, 1848, 118; truth about the fictitious signatures, 133.
Popular literature forty years ago, 6. 77; of the present day, 317.
Powell, the Home Office spy, 150, 166.
Prest, Thomas, song writer and novelist, 86.
Prince Consort, the report of his arrest, 266.
Privileges of Parliament, a breach of the, 248.
Provincial journalism and journalists, 239.
——— newspaper proprietor, conversation with a, 241.
Public Schools Commission and the *Times*, 253.

Rational Society, collapse of the, 62.
Reform Bill, Lord John Russell's, 244; Mr. Gladstone's, 293; Mr. Disraeli's, 310.
——— Conference in St. Martin's Hall, 208.

Roatan, a story of a blunder, 28
Roebuck, John Arthur, and Chartist movement, 98.
Rose, one of the conspirators 1848, 151, 165.
Russell, Lord John, and Pa mentary Reform, 244.
Rutland, Duke of, and the volun movement, 277.

Salisbury Square school of fict 89.
Schapper, Carl, a refugee artist,
Schleswig-Holstein, a diplom puzzle, 303.
Scripture readers' associations, 221.
Seven Dials, projected barricade 165.
Stephens, Joseph Rayner, no Chartist, 114.
Strike and outbreak of 1842, 35
Sunday question in Parliament in Hyde Park, 256.

Taylor, John, the Philhelle 102.
——— Peter Alfred, a letter fr 118.
Tillotson, John, author and jour ist, 231.

Urquhart, David, and the For Affairs Committee, 103, 108 denunciation of the author, his prediction of peace, in 1 305; connexion with the u montane Romanists, 313.